Praise for

Homeschool Co-ops: How to Start Them, Run Them and Not Burn Out

"I first knew Carol Topp as a fellow homeschool mom in our local support group. I knew then that she was sharp, but my respect for her grew to a whole new level when years later she became my CPA! Carol comes with wisdom and understanding of the homeschool movement as well as expertise in the field of accounting. I'm glad to see Carol share her talents and experience."

—Linda Lacour Hobar
Author of *The Mystery of History*

"Carol's expertise in accounting, coupled with her long-time acquaintance with the home-schooling movement, has proven invaluable to our organization. I only wish I had the information presented in this book years ago when we were first starting out on this adventure!"

—Mary Hood,
Author of *The Relaxed Homeschooler* and founder of
ARCHERS for the Lord, Inc. (Association of Relaxed Christian Home
Educators), www.archersforthelord.org

"This book is a fantastic resource for every co-op. There is some wonderful advice for situations that your group may encounter. A must read for new groups or those that have been around for quite awhile!"

—Kathie R., Kingdom City, MO
Kingdom Homeschool Association Member

"This insightful and practical book is a must-read for every leader (and member) of a homeschool co-op or support group. The Biblically-based guide is packed with helpful advice from experienced homeschool leaders who, like good friends, warmly share their wisdom and knowledge. It is a comprehensive resource that you will surely find yourself referring to again and again over the years."

—Teri O., New River, AZ
www.KnowledgeHouse.info

Homeschool Co-ops:

How to Start Them, Run Them and Not Burn Out

Carol Topp

Aventine Press

Homeschool Co-ops: How to Start Them, Run Them and Not Burn Out

Scripture taken from the HOLY BIBLE, NEW INTERNATIONAL VERSION®. Copyright © 1973, 1978, 1984 International Bible Society. Used by permission of Zondervan. All rights reserved.

ISBN: 1-59330-533-8

Library of Congress Number: 2008925392

Printed in the United States

Cover design by Dave Huff

Author Photo by Cathy Lyons, Lyons Photography

Disclaimer and Limitation of Liability

This book is designed to provide accurate and authoritative information about the subject matter covered. The author is not rending legal, accounting, or other professional advice.

The fact that a company, organization or website is mentioned does not mean that the author endorses the information or services provided. The resources mentioned in this book should be evaluated by the reader. Readers should also be aware that organizations and web sites mentioned may have been changed or ceased operations since the publication of this book.

Every effort has been made to contact cited quotes for permission of use.

Author Acknowledgements

I would like to thank all the homeschool co-op leaders from whom I have learned so much. Some I have had the privilege of meeting in person, and some I've only known virtually.

I appreciate my own co-op leaders—Melissa Owens, Laura Cripe and Mauren Rausch and board members—Cynthia, Kerri, Cathy, Kris, Julie, Michelle and Mary Jo. It has been such a pleasure serving with all you ladies.

Some of my fellow homeschool co-op members have been very helpful in editing this book. Without the Mason Co-op we would not have met! Thanks, Christy and Katie. You had the experience with formats, words, grammar and punctuation that I lack. Special thanks to my daughter Emily for her assistance in editing also.

Thank you to Dave Huff for the cover design and Cathy Lyons for the photo.

Thanks to my daughters, Emily and Sarah, and to my husband Dave, who supported me through writing this book. They always knew I had something to say!

And to Jesus, the world's greatest leader and our role model. I recall how many times our co-op has leaned on Him for wisdom, discernment and patience. He has never disappointed us!

Table of Contents

Introduction

What is a homeschool co-op?

A homeschool co-op is a group of homeschooling parents who join together to share teaching duties. These co-op parents need a source of helpful ideas, tips, and guidance. They want to know what others have done, what works and what doesn't. Individual homeschooling parents lack the time to search hundreds of web sites and read about how various groups began. Instead, parents need a single resource to help them out whether they are thinking about joining a co-op, wanting to start a co-op, or are already running a co-op.

How this book can help you

Homeschool Co-ops: How to Start Them, Run Them and Not Burn Out can help homeschool leaders manage a successful co-op. It discusses the benefits and disadvantages of co-ops. There is advice on **Starting a Homeschool Co-op** such as how to find potential members, how to organize, where to meet, and what problems to anticipate. This book also covers how to **Run a Co-op**. You'll read about daily operations for all size groups, conflict resolution, and volunteer management. This book also discusses legal and accounting issues for various co-op sizes such as taxes, budgets, collecting fees, and paying teachers.

Sprinkled throughout the book is advice from other homeschool leaders. Their advice can help prevent **burn out** and frustration. Experience has shown that having a board (or leadership team), some governing policies (formalized as bylaws and a policy manual) and an annual budget can all help prevent burn out of homeschool co-op leaders.

If you are thinking about starting a homeschool co-op or already leading one, you will find help on these pages. You can also visit my website **www.HomeschoolCPA.com** for more articles and resources on running a homeschool organization.

Carol Topp, CPA
Cincinnati, Ohio

Part One

Starting a Homeschool Co-op

Chapter One:
Benefits of Co-ops

"When my children were saying their bedtime prayers, they thanked God for our homeschool co-op," shared my friend Maren. "That's when I knew we'd be coming back next semester." Maren's children knew that co-op was special to them. They enjoyed seeing their friends, learning from other parents and participating in their classes. Their mother also benefited from belonging to a homeschool co-op. She received encouragement, support, information and made friends, too.

There are many benefits of being a part of a homeschool co-op. Some are readily apparent, and some show up after many months of involvement as relationships grow. I have been a member of a homeschool co-op for five years and my most valued benefits have been the friends that I have made and their support of my homeschooling efforts. I've shared burdens, ideas, and laughs. Obviously, from its very name, a co-op (from the word "cooperate") is a group of people working toward the same goal. I enjoy being with like-minded people once a week. It helps me to remember that I am not alone or isolated in my homeschooling experience.

Group Learning

One of the greatest benefits of belonging to a homeschool co-op is the opportunity for group learning. Many parents join a co-op simply to give their children some time in a group. Quite simply, children make friends at co-op. In my co-op, the students cannot wait for co-op day to arrive so they can see their friends. They may not realize it, but they can also benefit from learning from adults other than their parents. My daughters have been blessed to learn from talented, generous teachers. In addition, co-ops offer opportunities for group discussion and competitions.

Socialization

The most apparent benefit of a homeschool co-op is socialization. For years the homeschool movement has been criticized for the lack of opportunity to socialize. Critics believe that homeschooled children are isolated and need more interaction with their age-peers. The homeschool movement answers these critics in many ways. Sometimes we turn the question around and examine the unhealthy interactions occurring in many public schools. We proclaim that socialization is overrated and point out bullies, fights, disrespect, cliques, and so on as examples.

There are homeschoolers who are concerned about social interaction, and they seek out opportunities for their children to be a part of group activities. Thus we see the growth of homeschool sports leagues, classes, clubs, and of course, our focus, homeschool co-ops. These group activities balance the time spent learning alone or with the family. Most co-ops meet once or twice a week, therefore giving students a "taste" of group learning without being overwhelming.

Friends

My daughters have benefited greatly by belonging to co-ops because of the friends they have made there. Because of the Christian emphasis in our co-op, my daughters' friends come from like-minded Christian homes. I can honestly say that I am pleased with their choice of friends, many of whom are not all the same age. In our co-op, we group grades, typically three years, together. When in sixth grade, my daughter had friends in fourth, fifth and sixth grades. Unfortunately, I did not have that experience in my childhood. Most of my friends were exactly my age, until high school when I had friends different in age. Having friends two years younger was not considered "cool." How blessed my daughters are to be free of those social stigmas!

My neighbor and fellow homeschooler, Kirsten, was concerned about her oldest daughter making friends of her own. The daughter had been adopted from overseas as a teenager and was fitting into family life very successfully, but she didn't want to continue sharing friends with her siblings. I was so pleased to tell Kirsten about our homeschool co-op and the wonderful group of friendly high school students we had there. They visited the next week and joined immediately. I was thrilled when two weeks later, I saw Kirsten's daughter being hugged good-bye by other teenage girls. I looked over at my friend and said, "It's working!" and she wholeheartedly agreed. It warms my heart to see the excitement on co-op day as friends greet each other. Girls run and hug each other and boys smile as they see their buddies arrive. Of course adults also look forward to seeing old friends and making new acquaintances at co-op too.

Learning from Another Adult

Another social benefit children receive from a co-op experience is less readily apparent, but still extremely valuable: healthy relationships with other adults. The other parents who volunteer as teachers and helpers in our co-op serve as role models, mentors and teachers. I think it is very healthy for children to have adults they respect outside their own family. Sunday school teachers and Bible study leaders serve this role, and so can co-op teachers. I realize that I am not my children's only teacher. My children will learn from college professors and they will be exposed to trainers in the workplace someday. I want them to appreciate the different personalities that teachers possess. I also want my children to understand that they can learn from different types of people.

Children can greatly benefit from group study. The best source is homeschool co-ops. On the Bright Ideas Press website, owner Maggie Hogan shares some input from other veteran homeschoolers. One experienced co-op member, Beth, expresses this benefit of co-ops:

> Co-ops also require your children be accountable to someone other than mom or dad. In a co-op, children learn how to juggle many different teachers with different teaching styles. Co-ops allow your child to work in a group setting with children around their own age. They also learn to deal with "jerks", bullies, and other undesirable traits other children have (never our own children!). Teachers tend to put more effort into teaching groups of children than into teaching just one. These are just a few of the benefits I have found this year. I would never homeschool without co-ops again![1]

Group Interaction

When my daughter approached high school she wanted to discuss literature with someone other than me. She was right; it is awfully difficult to have group discussions without a decent-sized gathering! Co-ops provide a wonderful opportunity for your student to engage in group discussions and other classes. One mother, Debbie, recently enrolled her daughter in our co-op because we offered a book discussion class for high school students. She discussed how the class sounded like something her daughter needed. We also joked that the books sounded so interesting that we mothers wanted to attend the class too! Our co-op has held several classes that work best in a group setting including literature discussion, public speaking, gym games, and team building. One mother invented a class called Bee Alert where she had a different type of competition each week. Sometimes it was a spelling or geography bee, but she also branched out into Bible and history topics. These types of learning opportunities cannot be done as well in a home setting, but they work beautifully in a homeschool co-op.

Shared Experience of Teachers

Although co-ops offer the benefits of group learning to your children, you as their parent and teacher also reap rewards. You can use a co-op to share in the experiences of other parents. Because everyone has many varied gifts and interests, a co-op provides an outlet for the participating adults to use their talents to bless others. Your children can benefit greatly from taking a class with someone who has a passion for the subject as well as the experience to guide them.

Special skills

When I joined our co-op, I found a blessing in the Spanish teacher, Mrs. Tann, who majored in Spanish in college and is a volunteer teacher at our co-op. My daughter, Emily, had been learning Spanish from a computer program. Although she was doing well and making good grades on the quizzes, her Spanish greatly improved after starting Mrs. Tann's class. I noticed that she started speaking a few phrases and naming objects in Spanish. Mrs. Tann has Spanish skills that neither my husband nor I possess. The Spanish class experience was invaluable because he studied French, and I did not study a foreign language at all! Mrs. Tann has a passion for teaching students Spanish and believes that Christians will be better witnesses to the world's Hispanic population if we speak their language. She sees teaching Spanish as a ministry; she must, since she volunteers her time and talent!

Talents

My daughter Sarah loves Mrs. Lyons her art teacher at co-op. Art is a subject I could never seem to get around to teaching. Personally, I like art and even have some (small) talent in drawing and painting. I felt guilty for not "doing" art more often in our homeschool. Then we joined a homeschool co-op and met Mrs. Lyons! She has a marvelous talent for artistic expression in many forms. Her encouragement helps students find ways to improve their skills. We are thrilled that Mrs. Lyons uses her talent in this way. Like Mrs. Tann, she sees teaching art as a way to glorify God. We heartily agree!

Our family has benefited from women (and a few men) with a passion for teaching a particular subject as well as the skills and experience to teach it to others. I am reminded of the verse in I Peter 4:10:

As each one has received a gift, minister it one to another,
as good stewards of the manifold grace of God.

Of course, a co-op needs not only teachers, but administrators, decision-makers, prayer warriors and encouragers, to name a few. These talented people may not be given a specific job description, but can be found volunteering in the nursery, paying the bills, hiring teachers, and attending board meetings. Everyone can benefit when talented members share their gifts.

Encouragement

In addition to gleaning from the experience of teachers, another benefit of co-ops is the encouragement that they offer to homeschooling parents, particularly mothers. I had a friend say that she didn't think she would have made it through her first year of homeschooling without her co-op. It wasn't her children but she who needed the encouragement and support of other homeschooling mothers.

Continue Homeschooling

One co-op director that I know believes that if a co-op helps even one mother to continue homeschooling, then all the work has been worthwhile. Specifically, she tries to support parents of high school students, many of whom drop out of homeschooling because the subject material grows more difficult at the high school level. For example, some parents feel ill-prepared to tackle algebra and biology with their students. Our co-op tries to help these families by offering high school classes in foreign language, upper math and advanced lab science. Other co-ops in our area offer fun subjects such as photography, yearbook, drama and art to keep kids interested.

Mothers share burdens

Of course, it is not just parents of high school students that need support; parents of younger children need assistance also. Emulating another homeschool co-op, my co-op offers a room for mothers to "Chew and Chat," where we can eat and talk. More importantly, we share each other's burdens there. Although we sometimes offer suggestions and new ideas, we often are just a sounding board. Mothers feel free to share their homeschooling struggles in our Chew and Chat room, because this group understands them without condemnation. We also organize meals for a family in need and donate school supplies if a family is suffering a financial setback.

Exchange information

While co-op mothers may share burdens, they also exchange information. One of the best things about a co-op is the wonderful exchange of ideas. Not a week goes by that I do not hear one mother sharing with another about a new curriculum, program, class, or website! Almost all my best recommendations have come from co-op mothers. Sometimes I see one mother bringing in a textbook to share with another mother. It is wonderful and very encouraging to both parties! Recently another co-op mom showed me two bags of math games and curriculum that she had been given by other mothers in the co-op. Her fifth grade daughter was struggling with basic math facts and other mothers came to the rescue with manipulatives and alternative math ideas. She was thrilled that she could borrow these items to try out on her daughter without spending a fortune.

The encouragement mothers get from a homeschool co-op is frequently an unexpected bonus. While they may have joined a co-op for their kids' sake, they receive a blessing themselves. Encouragement, information and support are invaluable hidden benefits of joining a co-op.

Fun

In addition to the educational benefits of group learning, shared experience and encouragement, co-ops can be a lot of fun! Your students should have creative teachers and see co-op learning as enjoyable! Even so-called boring classes like math can be made playful when presented as a game. Another mom and I taught a Math Games class for 4th -6th graders. The first time we offered it, we had six children. The class size was just right and we had a great time. The next semester we doubled in size. I guess word got around that it was a fun class. Maybe it was during our end-of-semester program when each class member held up their favorite math game that they had played in class (chess, dominoes, tanagrams, paper games, card games, calculator games, etc.). Yes, even math can be fun.

Special Events

Many co-ops offer fun activities such as field trips and special events. I have seen co-ops offer talent shows, plays, and recitals. My own co-op has hosted Valentines Day events and Christmas parties as well as visits to a nursing homes, and Christmas caroling. One co-op is starting a 4-H club, while another has an American Heritage Girls troop and a Boy Scout troop. Going beyond these activities, some co-ops offer days at the beach, pool, park or ski slopes! The list is endless, and all in the name of fun and learning.

Because some events take more planning they can benefit from the many helping hands at a co-op. Science fairs, spelling bees, debate contests, and Bible or academic quizzes come to mind. Because parents are already gathered in one place weekly co-ops become an ideal venue for planning such activities. Additionally, the co-op probably has a variety of talents in their membership, which can provide the manpower. (See Chapter Seven "Co-op Offerings" for more ideas on activities a co-op can offer.)

The benefits of belonging to a homeschool co-op include —among others—group learning, experienced teachers, encouragement and fun. There are many more benefits that experienced co-op members could add to this list. Although some blessings are readily apparent in your children's faces, others develop over a longer period of time. Furthermore, some benefits you will not even acknowledge until your co-op experience ends and you realize that you are missing something. Regardless of the appearance of these benefits, I hope you gain all these advantages and more.

Chapter Two:
Disadvantages of Co-ops

Perhaps the last chapter on the advantages of homeschool co-ops has left you so starry-eyed that you are asking, "Are there disadvantages to belonging to a co-op?" Well, joining a co-op is a little like getting married. After the wedding and the honeymoon comes the marriage. Marriage is indeed a blessing, but it is best if you are well prepared and approach it with your eyes wide open. The same is true with homeschool co-ops. Life may be great for a while in your co-op with a harmonious group meeting all your expectations. Great! At this point you're on your honeymoon. Soon little annoyances may creep up, or things may not go the way you had expected. You may become disappointed. The honeymoon is over, with only the hard work of marriage (or co-oping) there to greet you!

Never fear. Like being married, the problems of co-oping can be resolved if you know what to expect. As a matter of fact, having unmet expectations is the number one complaint of dissatisfied former co-op members. In this chapter, I will discuss some of the disadvantages of co-oping.

Unrealistic or Unmet Expectations.

Like a spouse, no co-op will meet all your expectations. Before joining a homeschool co-op, you should examine your motivations and desires in joining a co-op. Ask yourself, "What is most important to me and my family? What do I want most out of this co-op experience?" As you contemplate these thoughts, I suggest you write them down.

What I want most from my co-op is:

_____

_____

Additionally, I'd like:

_____

_____

Perhaps you most desire social relationships for your children. Then when you are dissatisfied about the start time, the amount of homework or the lack of singing for preschoolers, focus on your strongest desire. Is that expectation being met? If so, release the other, lesser expectations.

When I joined a homeschool co-op, I wanted group interaction for my children as well as classes that I was not teaching at home, like art and speech. Since the co-op met those expectations, I was happy. On the other hand, some co-op members were not as satisfied with the experience. Among co-op members' varied expectations, some may be obvious and clear, while some of our hopes go unstated and often misunderstood.

One of our co-op members felt very strongly that our co-op should meet in a location close and central to all of our homes. In other words, her primary expectation was of a geographically tight community. While this may seem a bit Utopian with a group of 37 families, it was her desire. More importantly, she thought that others shared the same assumption. How disappointed she was when the co-op board decided to change locations! Our new location was not close or central anymore (but it was a great facility and less expensive). This member felt strongly enough about her hopes of being close geographically that she left our co-op after four years of membership and formed a small co-op of her own. Ultimately, this new co-op ended up a better situation for her because it met her expectations.

Surrendering Control

Ironically, surrendering control may seem like an advantage to some people who will gladly hand over certain subjects like algebra, biology dissection or foreign language. Of course, turning over teaching responsibility for difficult subjects can be a relief. In fact, access to advanced classes may be the reason you sought out a co-op to begin with!

While granting teaching responsibility to others may seem beneficial, turning over *control* is another matter. Face it: homeschoolers like control! We like to direct our children's environments, their exposure to the world, and their friendships. We pick carefully the curriculum they use. I once met a woman who really wanted *every* subject her child studied to be firmly grounded and rooted in Scripture including Bible verses for every chapter of science, etc. While this woman may have found her perfect curriculum for use at home (there are several to choose from), she would not have enjoyed a co-op because she would have had to relinquish some control.

If releasing control over certain subjects is an issue for you, then you can do one of two things: Release your hold, praying frequently, or find a co-op that will use the curriculum you desire. In Chapter Seven "Co-op Offerings," I discuss co-ops that are formed around particular curricula.

Different Styles

One year, I noticed my daughter coming home with a lot of crafts she had made at co-op. "Is this from your Ohio History class?" I asked, looking at a cute, painted clay bowl and a burlap-covered booklet she had made. "Sure, we're studying Ohio's Native Americans," she responded. Personally, I would have been spending more time on Ohio's Presidents. After all, Ohio is called the Birthplace of Presidents, claiming eight Presidents with origins in the state. Although I was not the teacher, in crept the thought, "I'd do it differently." Well, I was not in charge of the class. Another teacher had volunteered to teach Ohio History. In fact, my daughter enjoyed her class. I may not have liked another teacher's choices, methods, or materials, but I was not running the class, so I had to accept the teacher's decisions. As my pastor preaches, unless you are going to be part of the solution, do not be a part of the problem by criticizing. He also tells us, "It's not about *you*!" That little reminder should be posted at every co-op. The very word co-op (short for cooperation) means we are working together to accomplish a goal—home education, in our case. I do not always get my way at co-op because it is not all about me!

"Don't run! Don't bounce the ball inside! Stop kicking your sister!" I have been know to utter these commands while at co-op, and not just to my own children. I am one of those people who has no problem exerting authority over unruly children. After all, I am an adult, and we work together in our cooperative organization to keep everyone safe and peaceful. Conversely, I know that not everyone feels the way I do. Some people are extremely reluctant to discipline another person's child. Granted, I would never lay a hand on a child, but I do let them know if they are out of line. If you do not like assisting other parents in this way, or if you are very sensitive about other parents verbally disciplining your child, then you had better think carefully about a co-op commitment.

Socialization

Obtaining socialization opportunities and group interaction is often the primary reason a family joins a co-op. Unfortunately, socialization can also be a source of problems. First of all, remember that some children will be a terrific influence on your children. My daughter has made great friends at our co-op, and I am pleased with the friends she has. At the same time however, your son may be learning jokes you would rather not hear! Be prepared that not every student involved in your homeschool co-op is going to be a good influence on your child. Some co-ops address this by interviewing each child before enrollment. Although this practice has some merit, it is time consuming and unreliable. Some co-ops interview the parents, but I know several church-going, Christian parents whose children are wild! The faith or behavior of the parents is no guarantee that the children are little angels. Be aware that negative socialization can exist in a homeschool co-op just as it occurs in any school or large group setting.

Because of the potential for negative social interactions, you may need to spend some time after co-op discussing issues with your child. Remind your child what is acceptable behavior and language for your family. If a problem such as bullying, teasing, or foul language persists, bring it to the attention of the co-op leadership. You can read more about dealing with conflicts and problems in your co-op in Chapter Nine "Managing Volunteers and Conflict."

Time and Money Commitment

A commitment to joining a co-op will involve your time and money. First, there will be an investment of time on co-op day itself. If your co-op requires you to teach a class, it will take preparation time outside of co-op day. Joining a co-op means that others are depending upon you to uphold your commitment. If you do not show up at co-op one week, someone else will need to fill the gap. If you skip too many times, you may even be asked to leave the group! My family blocks out Friday mornings and early afternoons for co-op. That means we miss out on plays, classes and field trips offered on Fridays, but we stick to our commitment. One family could not rejoin our co-op when we moved from Thursdays to Fridays. The family took frequent three-day weekends and could not attend on Fridays. I miss that family, but I respect them for not joining the co-op when they knew they could not commit to being there every week.

In addition to a time commitment, co-ops require money. While most of the co-ops I am familiar with keep costs low, a co-op cannot run without charging some fees. Overall, I think co-oping provides tremendous benefits for the money, but some homeschoolers are financially strapped and find even a small fee difficult to manage.

There are homeschool organizations that hire teachers and do not require the parents to volunteer. There is a homeschool program in central Ohio that sees its purpose as relieving mothers of their educational responsibilities for a few hours a week. While this is an honorable goal, the cost of this program is significantly higher than a volunteer teacher at a homeschool co-op. Realize that you will pay with time, money or perhaps some of each.

Too Much Like School

Some co-ops have a very school-like structure. My co-op met in a building owned by a small Christian college. The rooms had chalkboards and desks, giving a very school-like feel. Many of our parents and teachers liked the building and classrooms because it was efficient to conduct classes in a schoolroom. If you are a free spirit or an unschooler, you may not feel comfortable in a classroom setting. Before joining, visit the co-op in action to get a sense of the surroundings and the environment. You may decide that the benefits outweigh the negative feelings of a structured environment, or you may conclude that you can live with a little structure once a week.

In a co-op class you might not be able to spend as much time on a subject as you might like. New York teacher John Taylor Gatto said it best in *Dumbing Us Down*:

> The third lesson I teach is indifference....When the bell rings I insist they drop whatever it is we have been doing and proceed quickly to the next work station. They must turn on and off like a light switch....Bells inoculate each undertaking with indifference.[2]

Homeschool co-ops like Mr. Gatto's public school are frequently structured around the almighty clock. We move kids to the next class on schedule so that they get the most out of their experience that day. When dealing with large groups, a co-op must rely on structure and timetables to keep things running smoothly. A small co-op or single subject co-op can be more flexible and free form. Decide for yourself how strongly you feel about being under a time constraint. The structure may even be a benefit to you or your children. In cases like this you can see how even potential challenges can ultimately benefit you and your children in your co-op experience.

Belonging to a homeschool co-op can have some challenges, but challenges can bring benefits. What is a disadvantage to co-oping for some people such as surrendering control, can be a benefit for another homeschooling mother. Some co-ops may seem too structured for one family, while another family could benefit from more organization in their lives. Joining a homeschool co-op will take commitment, but hopefully it will be time and money well spent.

It may not be problem-free to start or run a homeschool co-op, but most homeschool parents find that co-oping is worth the commitment and expense! Homeschool co-ops are becoming more and more popular because they are meeting the needs and expectations of homeschooling families. I hope you go into this adventure with a full understanding of the costs and benefits. In the following chapters you will read a lot of stories and advice from homeschool leaders. It is my hope you can learn from their experiences and lead a happy, successful homeschool co-op.

Chapter Three:
Different Types of Co-ops

Co-ops come in all sizes. Some are as simple as a gathering of two families to teach their own children. Others are medium sized, with about five to ten families. Because medium co-ops are still small enough to be intimate, everyone knows each other. The co-op may be able to meet in a home. By the time you assemble more than 10 or 12 families, you have what I consider a large co-op. The size of a co-op can influence many issues such as the need for formal structure, more detailed money management, written rules, and policies.

Small

Small co-ops usually have a single focus with its members sharing a common interest. Perhaps the children are all of a similar age, or possibly they all enjoy studying the same subject, like art. Typically these co-ops are usually limited enough to meet in someone's home, albeit a large home or at least one large room! Because of their size, small co-ops have an intimate, comfortable feel.

Frequently these small co-ops need no formal structure. Decision-making, finances and start-up are quite simple. The person who starts the group is usually the founder and leader all in one. While she may make all the decisions herself, she might instead use consensus to decide issues. Usually everyone gets an equal say in matters. A small size makes finances easy to manage. Sometimes money is collected for supplies, but no formal bookkeeping or accounting is performed. The small co-op may not even have a separate checking account. Often, financial matters are handled in cash. If you want to see how much money the co-op has made then just look in the envelope marked "Co-op" in the leader's desk drawer. It's that simple. An advantage of a small co-op is that it can be started in a very short amount of time, usually a few weeks. Conversely, it can end just as quickly. Whenever the leader decides she is finished co-oping, it dissolves. Frequently, the small co-op lives and dies on the founding leader's commitment.

One problem a small co-op may encounter is having to limit their group size. What if others are desperate to join? Do you allow them to come and expand the group? Or would you rather become exclusive for the sake of the current members? There is no right answer; each co-op is unique. While expanding a co-op is a joyful experience, growing from a small group to a medium group can come with some trials. With more families, you will need more organization. In addition, you'll need a larger space as well as someone to handle the money. Some groups purposely stay small frequently as a decision made by the founder or leader. If she is ready and willing to put in the effort to see the co-op grow, it probably will. On the other hand, if she has no desire to manage a larger group, then the co-op may stay small. Do not feel you must grow to be successful. Consider the reasons you formed a co-op to begin with. Focus on those goals. A co-op may not last forever. Your desire should be to look back on the co-op season with pleasant memories. Sometimes, dragging the co-op into another year of existence can be a mistake. If the joy of gathering is gone and the co-op is more work than pleasure, than it is time to let it die.

From co-op leader Robin Bray comes a wonderful story of how a small co-op evolved:

The first (co-op) began when two burned out homeschooling moms determined that they would not ever do any of those enriching activities they talked about with the children unless they set a consistent, weekly date and stuck with it. My sister Jeanne and I were the two desperate moms, and the kids were the five children we had between us. We decided that, bottom line, we were going to get together once a week and do *something* with the kids, if it was nothing but let them play educational games together. So we came up with something we called 'Learning Centers Day'. We decided to set up a few learning centers around Jeanne's kitchen table, living room and schoolroom. Then we would let the kids rotate from center to center. Some centers were one kid centers; others allowed for more. We loaded an educational game in the computer. That was one center. We placed a variety of books in (a) chair and called it 'The Reading Chair.' Center number two! We put the V-Tech laptop computer toy at a small desk, set up to review multiplication facts. There's three! I taught 'skip counting' for multiplication at one table, while she played a phonics or spelling game with a child at another. So, we had five centers. We rotated every 15 or 20 minutes. "Hey! That's not a co-op! That's just two sisters and a bunch of cousins visiting together" Well, you may see it that way, but we all got a lot out of it. However, that's not the end of the story.[3]

Robyn goes on to tell us about how her co-op grew when other homeschooling moms heard about their activities.

I don't even remember who our first addition to the group was. But whenever we were around other families, naturally we mentioned "Centers Day" and the kids talked about it, too. It was something we enjoyed, and they looked forward to it. We were constantly planning what we would do next, so it was a frequent topic of conversation. Pretty soon, other moms were asking us, "What is Centers Day?", and our group began to grow.

We asked the other families to bring their favorite educational games to share. We told the other moms, "Any time you have an activity you would like to plan, go for it. We'll just close down one of our regular centers to make room for something different." Centers Day was a very flexible event. It did depend upon the participation of all the moms, even if all one had to do was supervise a game or keep a couple of toddlers occupied with clay or crayons. After a couple of years of this, Jeanne decided not to continue having Center's Day at her house, so another one of our group, Ginger, decided to host it the next year. But, remember: *all it takes is two desperate, burned out moms to start a co-op.*[4]

Robyn's story shows how flexible and simple co-ops can be. Also, I admire how Robyn and her sister transitioned leadership when the time was right. Here is Robyn's final word of encouragement including a challenge:

You don't have to call it a 'co-op' if that stresses you out. You don't have to call it anything. But it'll be easier to talk about it if you have a name for it...Centers Day, Fun School, whatever! *I dare you!* I dare you to start a two mom co-op...and still be a two mom co-op after four months. Even if you want to contain it, I think it would be a hard thing to do. You'd have to guard your mouth all the time to keep it a secret...but then the kids would spill the beans. It would take the pressure off if you didn't even have a goal of growing...just get with another desperate mom or two and decide what the *bottom line* is going to be. We'll all be waiting to hear how your experiment turns out![5]

Robyn's challenge to keep your small co-op a secret is difficult. Homeschooling is growing and co-ops are very popular. The children like Robyn's children enjoy co-ops and so do the parents! Another homeschooling mother, Janine Calsbeek, shares her story about a slightly larger co-op with seven families. She explains how her co-op made decisions and how they successfully addressed a few problems that came up.

A couple of us called our friends and homeschool acquaintances and got together for one (only one!) brainstorming meeting. Our idea? To offer a series of classes taught by us. We figured our non-classroom-oriented kids might benefit from a stint with a larger group. They might learn things that work better when there are more kids around. Might inspire each other? Collaborate? Socialize? Part of the thought behind this co-op, too, was to offer choices, at least for the kids who cared the most. So we offered a story discussion class and mostly the older kids signed up, six of them. The group read, they talked. It was something new for at least 75 percent of the class, and it was a hit. Speech was another highlight, especially when Kristin, the teacher, donned outfits to not wear when interviewing for a job... and then there was the day she demonstrated uncool telephone manners.

And we ended up with seven families, which meant we had seven parents willing to teach a class, and seven classes to offer to the kids. After coming up with a schedule and class descriptions, we circulated them via e-mail. Certain classes were recommended for certain ages, with flexibility, and the kids got a week or so to sign up. We alternated the meeting site each week between the library in Orange City and a church in Sioux Center. That worked too. We began January 9—the slowest time of the year in the North. From 2:30 to 3:20, middle-school-age and older kids met for speech or wildlife rehab class. The little ones, ages two to seven, attended A Day at the Pond. Then at 3:20 there were new classes and more choices. The young ones again got an animal theme, this time the farm variety, Green Acres. Those age eight and up chose between story discussion, putting together a newspaper and quilting.

The co-op hasn't been without its challenges. At least one parent would rather not do any teaching, and instead hire the teachers. She has six kids and is busy enough, she said. For most of us, the challenge of adding one more thing to the schedule—the co-op—was worth it. But we have options, like hiring a college student to teach instead. It's also not easy to find a time slot that works, especially with teenagers' schedules. A couple of kids wanted to take two classes that were offered in the same period. We just couldn't rearrange the schedule to accommodate everyone. And the youngest ones seemed to need a little more 'recess' than had been originally scheduled. No nursery was needed this time, but that's another problem that's easily solved.

The benefits dominated. I loved working with the kids on projects, hearing their multitudes of ideas and seeing them follow through. And I loved reading their writing, looking at their photos and listening to their speeches, being part of their debate and their laughter. Will we do it again? Definitely. We already have a list for next winter of at least three families so far who are definitely on. [6]

Janine's co-op started out fairly small, but at a level of organization that was manageable. I hope that from her story as well as Robyn's experience that you see how easy it can be to start a small homeschool co-op. The following chapters will help you get off to a good start. If you find your co-op becoming popular and outgrowing its small-size status, the following section will help you manage a medium sized group.

Medium

A medium-sized co-op (from five to about twenty families) has many advantages, the first of which being the ability to bless more people with the co-op experience! Besides members, leaders can gain rewards also. Obviously, a medium co-op has more hands and as we know, "many hands make light work." There are more families to carry the load. Frequently the newly added families bring in fresh ideas. Their contagious enthusiasm can rejuvenate a tired leadership team. Furthermore, some medium-sized groups find they can add new programs, such as field trips, advanced classes or dramatic plays. Perhaps one of the new members will use her talents in teaching a new class or writing a newsletter. At the same time, remember that medium groups will face additional challenges in communication and organization in proportional to their growth.

Organization

A medium co-op will need a bit more structure and organization than a small co-op. Make use of the newly added members by delegating responsibilities. Ask someone to serve as a treasurer. They should open a checking account for the co-op (see Chapter Eight "Money Management" for details). Additionally, a medium co-op may need registration forms to keep data straight. Ask a detail-oriented person to organize your paperwork. You may also need a simple policy manual. Decisions should not be made on impulse, but be carefully thought out beforehand. Turn to Chapter Six "Leadership" to get started.

Communication

Once a group reaches about a dozen families, it ought to consider communication via written newsletters, e-mail perhaps a website. Some groups use a free Yahoo Group to communicate. One co-op leader, Laurel Jew says,

> Communication is crucial, and we work at it through monthly board meetings and lunchtime Mom's Meetings. This year we added a 'Get Acquainted' potluck to which dads were invited... so they'd have some idea who their families were hanging out with all year! Through our members-only email loop and web site we post our syllabi, roster, schedule, homework, field trip invitations, and reminders about supplies for next week. Board members have a separate email loop for discussing group issues. Our co-op covers three different area codes and two counties. I find it hard to even imagine how we'd cope without email.[7]

Limited ages/grades

Frequently a medium co-op, although larger than a small co-op, cannot offer a full program. They must still limit their offerings in some way, either ages, grades or topics. Double Digits co-op in Ohio limits their students to children ages 10 and up (hence the name Double Digits). This helps them stay focused as they do not have to worry about staffing a nursery or offering a elementary classes.

Location

A medium co-op faces one of its greatest challenges in finding a meeting space. A small co-op can frequently meet in a home (albeit a large one!). Even in a large home however, a gathering of more than five families will feel crowded. If you grow to more than 10 families, you will be looking for a larger meeting space. Most groups turn first to free space in a library, community center, or church.

Churches are a very popular choice for medium sized co-ops. Usually churches are generous if a member asks for building space; they are supportive of families and education. Best of all, the building is sometimes empty midday when the co-op meets. In exchange however, some churches will charge a fee. After all, they have to pay utility bills and a janitor to clean up after you. If your co-op is strapped for cash (and most are), you can try to negotiate with the church. Offer to clean the bathrooms, take out the trash, and clean the floors after co-op each week in exchange for free or reduced rent.

Before volunteering your co-op families for janitorial duties, understand this comes at a cost. Many families are tired and want to go home after co-op, not stay to clean up. Mothers with babies and preschoolers find it difficult to vacuum the floors at home, let alone a large meeting room. Many co-ops have families take turns with clean up. Each family may have to clean up only once or twice a year. Our co-op did this for two years. We thought it was working well, until mothers complained that they were at the church for two to three hours after co-op doing the cleaning. Then, the church complained about the state of the boys' bathroom and blamed our group for a broken sink. We paid for a new sink and started looking for a new location.

Some co-ops find that paying for clean up either to their landlord church or to a cleaning team is worth the money. One group hires a member to clean up after them each week. The co-op pays her $50 a week and she is happy for the income. Other groups work out a "volunteer or pay" system. If a family cannot volunteer to clean up, then they pay $25 - $50 instead. This way the co-op hires someone to do the cleanup instead of the assigned family. The simplest but most expensive solution is to pay the church's maintenance crew for clean up. The expense is usually included in the rental fee. My church prefers this arrangement with outside groups. As a matter of fact, they do not allow groups using the building to move chairs, setup, or clean up. It seems to work better for everyone if the professionals are just left to do their jobs since they know the building and how to use the commercial-grade cleaning equipment.

Several subjects

With a medium-sized homeschool group, you can offer a greater selection of classes. You may decide to expand from a single focus, such as science, to include literature or history as well. Robyn Bray writes about a medium- sized monthly co-op that was organized around different topics and activities. Her story is inspiring because it opens the co-oping model to new ideas. While this co-op met only once a month, every meeting was a different topic. The co-op, although medium-sized, was still flexible, allowing Robyn's family to come when they could.

This type of co-op requires a little more commitment from its members. Each family, upon joining, commits to planning one or two events in the upcoming season. How many events each member must commit to depends on how often the co-op plans to meet and how many members are in the group. For instance, if your co-op has 12 families, and you intend to plan one event per month, then each family would need to commit to being in charge of one event for the 12-month year. Or, if you wanted to have two events per month over a 9-month period, each family would need to be responsible for 1 or 2 events.

For the last year or so, I've been involved in this type of co-op. The first year, I withdrew early in the year, as my mother-in-law was very ill and I didn't know how long our family would need to stay free to be available for her care. The co-op coordinator told me I need not withdraw, just come when I could. She told me, 'You really only have to commit to the session you are in charge of. We can sign you up for a slot later in the year.' But I did not yet understand the level of freedom such a co-op permits, so I dropped out.

Some of the activities this co-op has enjoyed are:

- a trip to nearby planetarium
- a session on manners at one member's home
- a session on simple machines, with centers set up to demonstrate and experiment with each type of simple machine
- a study on wheat, including making pretzels and planting wheat
- a visit to a local nursing home during December to sing Christmas carols
- a session on gun safety and seeing police dogs at local military base
- a session on manatees, which included video clips, taking notes, and poetry.

While the older kids are taking notes, the younger may be doing a word search puzzle with words related to the topic of the day. Coloring sheets or a simple craft are also good ideas for the younger children. Of course, stories, poems, songs, and many games can involve all ages.

One absolute for this type of co-op is that it is *not* a babysitting service. All children must be accompanied by a parent, and each parent will need to help out during the session. While the hostess of the day does a more difficult activity with the older kids, someone else may need to help with a craft for the younger kids. Each child thus enjoys the group interaction, and the parents are able to support both the hostess and their own children in the activities. This way, it's much easier to maintain order and make the event a more pleasant experience for all. Besides, getting to know each other better is an important part of the co-op experience.[8]

Robyn's mid-sized co-op did require a little more organization and planning than a small co-op, but they used their larger size to offer more programs. They also used the advantage of their medium size to offer a larger selection of classes. Medium sized co-ops offer a lot of flexibility while not being too difficult to manage. The next section will cover the unique challenges of a large homeschool co-op and its advantages also.

Large

Large homeschool co-ops of more than ten families require more formal structure, money management rules, and written policies. A large co-op is characterized not only by its size, but also by its offerings. While these bigger groups will encounter some new challenges, they will also see many more opportunities.

Offerings

Large co-ops have the advantage of offering many different subjects and activities to their members. While this is a great benefit, it also means that there are more details to manage, such as teacher and room assignments. I've seen large co-ops that offer up to four choices of classes for every age group. Their class list is a delightful smorgasbord of educational opportunities. If you wish for a strong academic focus, you can probably find it in a large co-op. If, instead, you like to keep your co-op experience fun and lighter academically, there are probably art, music and game classes for you, too.

Debra Bell, an experienced large co-op leader, explains how co-oping with other homeschoolers met her need for academic subjects at the high school level.

Cindy and I had been co-oping for years, but our co-op was primarily extra-curricular type stuff and supplemental to our core program. Our new idea was to offer full-credit courses that would provide a framework for all the work students would do in that subject area throughout the school year. Plus, I was looking for an out from teaching any more math or science - I'd had my fill. What I really wanted was time to teach the literature I loved and to develop young writers - my passion. As perplexing as this was to me, we had another friend, Vickie, who was dying to have someone else teach English so she could devote herself to science classes (yuck!). And then we had another friend, Jane, who really wanted to coach Math Olympiad teams and teach kids math problem-solving strategies. Wow, instead of our kids benefiting from our strengths, and suffering from our weaknesses; we decided to pool our passions, talents and resources so all of our kids could have teachers who actually cared about their subject matter and knew what they were talking about most of the time.[9]

Debra's co-op, called CHESS—an acronym for Creative Home Educators Support Services—eventually grew into a well-structured large co-op with a board, administrator, hired teachers and formal policies. She goes on to comment:

During my travels, I've seen a lot of different co-ops in operation, and we all organize ourselves a bit differently. We can really benefit from sharing our experiences with one another. The important point, though, is that co-operative classes, especially on the high school level, are an excellent way to meet genuine academic needs without giving up parental oversight of our children's education.[10]

One of the primary benefits of a large co-op is the wide selection of classes that can be offered (see Chapter Seven "Class Offerings" for more ideas of high school classes offered at homeschool co-ops). This is usually the enticement /incentive for parents to join a co-op. Offering academic classes at the high school level also fulfills others' needs and expectations. It encourages homeschooling though high school if the family desires. High school level classes also provide social opportunities for teenagers without friends becoming too strong a focus in their lives. However, a wide array of classes may attract more families to your co-op meaning that you will need more structure and policies to manage a larger group.

Structure

When California homeschooling mother Laurel Jew started the Liberty Classical Academy she had five families. By the second year they had reached 13 families, and found they needed more structure.

> More families meant more students, but also more help. We rearranged classes to keep things participatory—not a drop-off or play program—making sure every mom had teaching responsibilities. New families fit fairly smoothly into the preschool and art teaching slots, at first with one of the original five members as 'backup.' In Year Two we learned logistics like printing a schedule for each table, starting an email loop, and what kind of lunches were easiest. We also met a code enforcement officer (35 kids in a park on a school day are a bit conspicuous), and found families would come and go but we needed to offer grace to all—and insist on timeliness. We learned to bring extra toilet paper and that even in California there are days you want to be inside!

> This year every class officially has a syllabus and a primary teacher, alternate teacher, and helper, that's 3 classes per mom, although those with toddlers participate in only two classes each. We built in three-level backup to allow for sudden illness, vacations, discipline issues at the park, and even potty breaks. It also keeps us moms from distracting others. Everyone is committed to being present on time, all day, with chit-chat limited to lunchtime (this works better, we found, when everyone is busy).[11]

If after reading stories like Laurel's you need more help with structure, then see Chapter Six, "Leadership," which discusses forming a board and writing a policy manual in detail.

Location

Typically, a large co-op accommodates all ages from birth through high school. You will need a meeting space that can accommodate children of all sizes. One year, a church offered its facility to our co-op. The location was convenient, the price affordable and the pastor agreeable. The only problem was the lack of rooms for the junior and senior high school students. They would have had to meet in separate corners of the fellowship hall. As this situation was less than ideal, we were forced to decline their offer and kept looking for a better facility. While searching for a meeting place, remember also to consider the needs of babies and toddlers. They need a safe environment preferably with cribs, swings and toddler toys. Additionally, a large co-op may need a large gathering space. Churches work well for many large co-ops because the sanctuary or gym can be a spot to assemble for announcements as well as a place for drama or gym class.

As you search for a large location, you'll discover that space comes at a premium. Most large co-ops find that they must pay rent. Consider this expense when making out a budget for the year. In addition to rent, you may have extra expenses in the form of cleaning supplies, trash bags, paper and office supplies. I discuss budgeting for these expenses in Chapter Eight, "Money Management."

Many landlords, even if they are churches, want groups using their facilities to purchase general liability insurance. This type of insurance provides protection against lawsuits involving bodily injury such as slips and falls, and damage to physical property. If your coffeemaker causes a fire, then the homeschool group may be liable for any damage to the church's building. Include insurance expenses in your financial planning also.

My homeschool co-op moved locations four times in six years, so we are familiar with the process of evaluating space and facilities for our co-op. Our co-op board created a checklist of items to consider when evaluating a co-op facility

Checklist for a Homeschool Co-op location and facility

What to look for in a facility for your homeschool co-op

- **Location, Location, Location**
  Easy access for most members
  Driving distance for most members
  Parking

- **Facility Space**
  Number of rooms
  Condition of rooms
  Nursery
  Preschool
  Elementary
  High School
  Lunch room
  Gym
  Gathering place
  Storage
  Bathrooms

- **Cost**
  Monthly rent
  Insurance needed?
  Utilities included?
  Phone included?
  Use of building's equipment included?
      Refrigerator/ Microwave
      Copier
      Sound/Audio/Visual equipment
  Any additional expenses (repair, maintenance, etc...)

- **Relationship with Landlord**
  Supportive of homeschooling
  Co-op member also church member (if landlord is a church)
  Personality of contact person
  Availability of contact person
  References from previous tenants

- **Extra Duties/Issues**
  Clean up requirements
  Set up requirements
  Use policies (any areas off limits?)

I hope this checklist provides some items for your consideration when searching for a co-op meeting place. There are many factors to consider. Your leadership should discuss the importance each of the factors listed above might be to your co-op members. My co-op found that cost and the relationship with the landlord were very important to the board since we are the ones dealing with the landlord. The need for a supportive landlord is not understood by most of the membership at large, because members tend to focus on distance and comfortable, clean rooms. I encourage you to focus on the needs of the co-op at large when visiting potential locations.

Volunteers or paid teachers

Homeschool co-ops come in all shapes and sizes, and there really is not one correct way to run a co-op. I have heard some leaders describe "true" co-ops as being 100% volunteer-based with mothers doing all the teaching. Conversely, I would not think you had fallen in esteem if your group hired a paid teacher. I think variety is the spice of life, and I am amazed at the creativity of homeschool parents to use co-ops to meet their academic needs. My own co-op hires a few paid teachers. We also allow high school students to be dropped off (meaning a parent does not stay and volunteer). These options seem to work for us as we keep a mix of paid and volunteer teachers. There are other programs however that lean heavily upon paid teachers. My daughters started attending a home school extension program when they entered high school. This program is run with all paid tutors that conduct classes for homeschool students twice a week. It became very popular and outgrew its location when it reached 125 students and now meets in two locations enrolling almost 200 students.

Co-op member, Debra Bell, discusses some advantages of having paid teachers and how her group's leader handles them.

> It's all well and good to use folks who volunteer their services. However, it is easier for a volunteer to withdraw her services or fail to follow through than it is for someone being fairly compensated for her contribution. Again, bartering classes and other benefits that do not cost money is often a good arrangement. Cindy (the co-op's co-leader) has wisely elected to make teachers her employees. I've seen other situations where the co-op administration simply serves as a broker of sorts for anyone in the area wanting to offer classes. These teachers then set their own fees, determine which students they will take, and function fairly autonomously. Cindy wanted to have final say on class content and the philosophy of education that permeates CHESS. This has allowed for a consistency throughout our program and, I think, long-term satisfaction for our families. It also gives Cindy the latitude to ask teachers to make adjustments where necessary, because she is clearly the person in charge.[12]

A large, formal group like CHESS needs structure. Their leader showed foresight and planning in hiring the paid teachers as employees. She knew the advantages of control, consistency and focus on the mission of the co-op were important. You can read more about volunteers and the issues of hiring and paying employees in Chapter Nine, "Managing Volunteers."

Not All Things for All People

Although bigger homeschool co-ops can offer more, even a large co-op cannot be all things to all people. For example, your co-op may offer all grades, but be limited on size. One such group is The Learning Tree Co-op in Ohio which has a waiting list every year. New members are allowed to join only if they can teach a class. They cannot grow larger because their co-op is sponsored by a church and they receive free space and invaluable support from the church. Since they fill the facility on co-op day and cannot add another family, they must turn away families every year. Being unable to join that co-op prompted one homeschooling mother, Melissa Owens, to start another co-op, which became the one I joined! Thus blessings can result from a seemingly bad situation. As a leader you should not feel guilty for limiting your group size. Someone else will step forward to fill the need.

Paula, a co-op leader, had tears in her eyes as she told her story. She desperately wanted to help the mother of an autistic son. Being a softhearted woman, Paula wanted to allow the boy into her homeschool co-op. The board viewed things differently however. They saw the potential drain on the volunteer teachers, the distraction to the other children, and the loss of focus on the co-op's purpose that would occur if this boy were allowed to join. With regret, they had to explain to the mother that this co-op was not suited to her son's needs. The group had to keep their focus as they were successfully serving 80 families. That was their calling, and they wanted to continue in that path. "I learned that, regretfully, we cannot be all things to all people-only Jesus can," Paula shared at our leader's support group meeting.

Ramona in Minnesota had a similar situation with special needs families in her co-op. She confirms that a single group cannot be all things to all people with her own experience.

> You, as leaders, need to set very clear parameters about what you want your co-op to be or not be. This is not mean-spirited or exclusionary, but instead is creating a specific ministry to meet specific needs. If you want an academically challenging,

true co-op, then set it up that way, and let someone else create a drop-in center. Quite frankly, a paid teacher, tuition-based co-op is *much* harder to run, since the level of administrative stuff goes up exponentially. When folks feel they've paid for a service, they are much more apt to complain about it, whereas if they are responsible for the outcome, they have to fix it themselves!

Sometimes it gets uncomfortable having to "winnow" and deny some families, but it's easier than dealing with the emotional drain that a poor choice can bring. Always keep in mind that you cannot be all things to all people, and that someone else will fill the niche you've left open. Academically, we teach to the highest level students, and let the others audit or accommodate them in some way. Ironically, although we do have many learning-disabled students, and they do well with us, some of our co-op members left and started a new co-op geared toward special needs kids. There was no rancor or hard feelings, it has been a good deal for everyone! (I teach at both now!) So, a ministry was created by our maintaining a narrow focus.[13]

Ramona's story of another co-op group forming because they saw a need and decided to meet it is very inspiring. I hope you too see yourself and your co-op as meeting some important needs in your homeschooling community. Whether your co-op is small, medium, or large, it has a unique purpose and role to fulfill. The next two chapters on organizing a planning meeting and defining your purpose will help you decide many important issues such as your co-op's goals and mission.

Chapter Four:
Your First Planning Meeting

You have decided to take the plunge: you are going to start a homeschool co-op! Good for you. Your efforts and willingness to take initiative will be a benefit to many homeschooling families. Hopefully you understand that the benefits of co-oping far outweigh the disadvantages. I hope that you have been inspired by some of the stories from Chapter Three and have started contemplating your co-op's unique purpose. The next chapters on planning and finding a mission will help you determine the specific characteristics of your co-op. A good way to start is by thinking through your first planning meeting.

Gathering Help

In this and the following chapters I will make several recommendations. Treat these as *suggestions* based on my personal experience and reading from others' knowledge. These are *not* rules; there is no "one way" or "correct way" to start or run a homeschool co-op. I have read many web sites about starting a home school co-op that state specific rules, such as "Do not let your co-op be more than five families." That may be good advice if you want a small co-op, but it is not applicable to everyone.

Flexibility is one of the beauties of homeschooling. You have the freedom do what is best for you, your family and your homeschool group. Since I do not know your particular needs, I could not properly tell you what to do. Since I am merely offering advice I will try to keep the "do it my way" attitude to a minimum. Now for my first bit of advice…

First of all, *do not do this alone*! Having a small group of people to help you is absolutely essential in running a successful homeschool co-op. Some people say, "If you want something done right, you have to do it yourself." That kind of thinking will be to your detriment because you will burn out. You may even regret the day that you thought you wanted to start a homeschool co-op. In order to counteract this desperation, you need other like-minded people to share this burden. Before announcing the start of a new co-op, gather help and seek out people who might be interested in a co-op as members or leaders.

There are several ways to find families interested in starting a homeschool co-op. Many co-op leaders started out very small with only a few friends and with a short-term commitment of only one to two months. A short-term commitment allows everyone involved to see if they like being a part of the co-op. Before you begin, have a definite closure to the trial co-op so that families can feel comfortable leaving if they wish. If enough families enjoyed the short-term experience, then they may be open to planning a longer term co-op experience of several months. During this time, you can also determine members' strengths and gifts. Some parents may enjoy leadership while others may prefer classroom teaching or assisting.

Another way to find co-op partners is to talk individually to other homeschooling parents. Call or e-mail them and ask, "Have you ever belonged to a co-op? Would you like to be in one? Would be interested in helping me start a new group?" When you ask for their help, be sure to emphasize the reason you called them. Emphasize their talent, experience or personality such as "You're always so calm," or "You're so organized that I know you'd be a great help to me." Who can resist an honest compliment? Also seek out parents that have belonged to a homeschool co-op before. Their experience will prove very valuable.

Some homeschool co-ops start when the leader makes a general invitation. A few years ago, a homeschooling mother with co-op experience sent out an e-mail to my homeschool support group stating she was having an information night about the possibility of starting a co-op in our area. She invited any interested parents to attend. About ten homeschooling mothers showed up that night, and I was one of them. Ironically, I decided not to become involved in that co-op because I thought my children were too young at the time. Eventually I did join this co-op and still belong five years later!

On the other hand, be aware of the potential problems in making a general invitation at this early stage. You will receive lots of ideas, both good and bad! You may encounter strong personalities who dominate your group with their opinions, possibly killing the group before it is born. I recommend that you save the large-group invitation until after you have made some basic decisions and can answer common questions. I suggest you start with a small group of three or four interested parents. Work out the details of time and place. Then announce to the entire homeschool community the exciting news that a new homeschool co-op is starting. This chapter on planning and the following chapter on finding a mission should be discussed and solidified in a small group of leaders, not a large body. Here is some great advice about gathering help from Nancy Carter, a veteran homeschool parent and group leader:

> I'd just say to really pray about it and to pray that God would guide you and affirm any decisions by bringing enthusiastic volunteers. Each group is so different with different needs & dynamics. People are all in different seasons of their lives. Start out by thinking what would really be great for your family and then let your group know what you're willing to do. You can't please everyone, but if you are pleasing the Audience of One that's all that really matters.[14]

Nancy has excellent advice about determining what your family desires in a homeschool co-op. Here is a short exercise to get you started thinking about your individual needs and your willingness to serve. You might want to copy and hand out this short survey to a handful of potential helpers. Their answers will help you discern who is willing to help you start a homeschool co-op.

What do my family and children need from a homeschool co-op experience?

_____

_____

_____

What do we NOT need?

_____

_____

_____

What am I willing to do?

_____

_____

_____

What am I NOT willing to do?

_____

_____

_____

Potential helpers:

Name	Talent/Experience	Phone/e-mail	Response

Decisions, Decisions

Once you have gathered some like-minded people, set out some cookies and coffee and get to work! I recommend you print up a simple agenda like the one following, and hand it out to every person attending. Having a plan will keep you on track and focused on making basic decisions.

It will be very easy to digress as people share ideas and expectations. Most likely you may find your group trying to focus on too many details, sometimes called "majoring in the minors." At this preliminary point you are working on the big picture, the basic issues. Leave the details for a later meeting. Get used to saying, "We'll postpone that discussion for a later meting," and then write yourself a note to that effect.

Some groups mistakenly tackle an issue that should be considered and discussed outside of the group meeting. One example is location. Assign one person to seek out a location and report what she finds. The entire group may go and see the chosen building, but only one person needs to do the initial scouting.

Expectations

Before your meeting, do some initial planning by asking the attendees to share their expectations with you. Use a form like the one following, and either e-mail it or ask the questions directly to potential members. I think the answers will be very revealing. If there is a consensus of needs and expectations, then you have a great start and can move ahead swiftly. Conversely, if there are conflicting needs or expectations, then you will need to discuss those issues before progressing. Here is how one homeschool group gathered input on the expectations of their members:

> When our group was just getting started, with about 20 families, one thing we did at a parent meeting was to make a "wish list"—what things would you like a support group to do or offer? There was no promise that our group would do these things, but I wrote them all down on a white board as we talked, and then published the list in our newsletter. It was really helpful to see what people wanted from a group; and over the next several years, just about everything on that list came to be![15]

Expectation Worksheet:

What do my family and children *need* from a home school co-op?

_____

_____

What do we NOT need?

_____

_____

What do I hope for as a *result* of belonging to a home school co-op? (friends, support, academic classes, etc.)

_____

_____

_____

Notice that this exercise focuses on needs and results, not the "nitty-gritty" of when and where. In thinking and talking initially about needs and hopes, you will focus on the main goal of your co-op instead of getting lost in the details. You can read more about goals in Chapter Five "What's in a Name? Names, Missions, and Purposes."

Agenda for First Planning Meeting

Expectations: If you have gathered results beforehand, summarize them here or record expectations during the meeting.

Common expectations: _____

Four W's and H:

- What

- Who

- When

- Where

- How much

List of Initial Classes to Offer:

The Four W's and H

As you see on the sample agenda above, your group needs to discuss the Four W's—What, Who, When, Where and one H—How much. These are crucial issues to be determined early. I will elaborate a bit on each.

What

This topic addresses the question, "What will we do?" The goal in asking this question is to focus on a particular mission. Since you cannot be all things to all people, you must focus your mission. Chapter Five, "What's in a Name? Names, Missions, and Purposes," will help your group focus on a mission statement which will probably require another meeting to discuss fully. For now, discuss broad, general ideas. Use the expectation worksheets to find a common goal. Put off the discussion for the next meeting if it goes too long or if there are vast disagreements.

For your first planning meeting, aim to come up with a general list of classes that you would like to see offered initially. Your group size, mission, and age focus will help you focus on a list of classes. If your co-op is fun-oriented then your classes might include Art, Music, Drama and Crafts. If you are academically focused, you might have Math, Spanish, and Creative Writing. Try and come to agreement on a few classes. You can focus on specific curricula later.

Who

Discuss whom your co-op will focus on. Will it be age restricted? Some co-ops want to offer classes and activities for elementary students while others focus on junior and senior high school students. Most co-ops focus on entire families from nursery to grade 12. Will your co-op be limited to those with a shared faith? Many homeschool co-ops develop a statement of faith for their group. I discuss statements of faith in Chapter Six "Leadership".

Do not feel pressured to accommodate everyone. You simply cannot meet everyone's needs. You will be more successful and avoid burn out if you can define your target group from the beginning. Inevitably, some people may complain if their desires or wants are not met. Encourage them to start a group for their specific needs (hand them a copy of this book!)

When

Discuss when and how often you will meet. Most co-ops meet weekly, but some gather every other week or only monthly. In contract, some groups with high school academic subjects meet twice a week. Also discuss the day and time. Is morning best? Is afternoon better? Some groups prefer holding co-op in the afternoon because parents can still manage to get a little "school work" done in the morning. On the other hand, afternoon co-ops interfere with babies' and toddlers' naps. Furthermore, some co-op members find if they meet in the morning, the day is "shot" and parents cannot get the children to refocus on school subjects when they return home.

The day of the week for a co-op's meeting may be driven by availability of space. If the church that rents you space is available only on Fridays, then that is when your co-op will meet. The decision is made. Alternately, if you have a choice of days then you will need to discuss which day of the week is best. I am familiar with co-ops that meet on every day of the week (except weekends!). Some prefer Monday and start the week off that way; others prefer Fridays and end the week with co-op! There is no perfect choice, but when your co-op will meet needs to be discussed.

Also discuss the duration of the co-op. Will it meet for the full school calendar or only for a semester? Some co-ops meet for only six- or eight-week periods twice a year. This schedule gives everyone a break. If you are offering high school level classes for credit, you should probably consider a longer duration of 14 to 18 week semesters.

Where

Many co-ops meet in churches, libraries and parks. Naturally, the size of your group dictates the space needed. Perhaps your group is small enough to gather in a house, but beware of problems in meeting in homes. Too many unsupervised children can damage a house. Also be aware of pets in a home as they can trigger allergies. Since I am allergic to cats, my family could not participate in a co-op held in a home with cats. If you must search for a place, start with your members' connections in your community. You could ask for each member to approach two or three churches, libraries or community organizations that might have space.

Because all of the W's—What, Who, When, and Where—are interconnected, deciding one issue will influence the others. For example, if you want a family-oriented co-op for all ages, meeting weekly for three hours and expect 20 families, your space needs will be significant. If, instead, you limit your co-op to five families from your church and they all have children under ten years old, you could meet every other week at a park. Perhaps one parent can agree to hold a class in her home for an hour while everyone else is at the park. A co-op might decide to use the same book to study animals in a monthly science co-op. The possibilities are endless and can change as your group evolves.

How much

Early on in your planning meetings, you must discuss how much the co-op will cost. No one likes being surprised when it comes to paying bills. Naturally, the scope of your co-op will determine your expenses and the fees you will charge members. Some groups set a fee and then keep their expenses under the amount of fees collected. For example, a small co-op could keep expenses to a minimum by only charging $10 per family for supplies. Conversely, because a larger group must rent space, buy insurance, provide clean up, etc, they might calculate their total expenses and then divide them among all families equally.

Some co-ops charge fees by the family while others charge for each student. Although charging by the family is easier for your treasurer to track, charging by the student seems to work better for some co-ops. Furthermore some classes are more expensive than others. For instance, an art class usually involves more costs than a writing class. Should some parents pay an extra supply fee based on each class or should everyone pay the same amount into a general fund? Discuss these options. The Veritas Homeschool Co-op in Lebanon, Ohio charges a family fee and an additional fee for individual high school classes. This two-tier structure works for them and the possibilities are numerous.

Involve your treasurer in these discussions (I hope you have already asked someone to consider being a treasurer). His or her opinion on the fees charged should weigh heavily, since the treasurer will create the budget and control expenses. See Chapter Eight, "Money Management," for help in designing a budget. For your initial planning meeting, try to reach a consensus on what families are willing to pay. Determine what other co-ops in your area charge to get a feel for the market. After you make these basic decisions, the treasurer can create a budget.

Starting a homeschool co-op should not be a solo endeavor. You should begin by finding like-minded, gifted people to help you lead and make decisions. During your first planning meeting you will cover many important topics starting with a discussion of expectations. In addition the details of starting a homeschool co-op— What, Who, When, Where, and How much—should be firmed up. I hope you will feel a strong sense of accomplishment. These are important issues that will lead to a positive successful co-oping experience for both the leaders and the co-op members.

Chapter Five:
What's in a Name?
Names, Missions and Purposes

O Romeo, Romeo! wherefore art thou Romeo?

Deny thy father and refuse thy name;

What's in a name? That which we call a rose

By any other name would smell as sweet;

—*Romeo and Juliet* by William Shakespeare

Although Juliet hoped that Romeo's name would not define him, in reality names are meaningful. For your homeschool organization the choice of your name is very important in establishing your co-op's identity!

What's in a Name?

Dual Names

Your organization will probably have at least two names: a legal title and a Doing Business As (DBA) name. For legal purposes, a name should be very distinct so your group will not be confused with another co-op or a school. My co-op's legal name is Mason Ohio Educational Home School Organization. That is quite a mouthful. On our checking account we are called Mason Home School Co-op, while members know us simply as Mason Co-op. Why the difference? In the state of Ohio, use of the word "co-op" in a legal name is reserved for corporations who file under the Cooperative Corporation Law. The name co-op can be only used by an organization that follows Ohio's law's for co-ops. These usually apply to electric co-ops or rural co-ops involving things such as sharing profits, membership voting, etc. Since my homeschool co-op does not want to follow those guidelines, nor are we a corporation, we cannot use the word "co-op" in our legal name. In our DBA name, however, we use the word "co-op".

List some DBA names for your homeschool co-op here:

_____

_____

_____

_____

Legal Name

Why do you need a legal name? For one, your group needs a legal title to open a bank account. In addition, if you want to be recognized as a non-profit organization by your state, you will need a legal name.

Also, if you want to pursue 501(c)(3) tax exempt status as an Internal Revenue Service (IRS) recognized charity, you will need a formal name. I discuss nonprofit corporation and 501(c)(3) status in Chapter Ten.

You may first encounter the need for a legal name when you apply for an Employer Identification Number (EIN) from the IRS. EINs are needed to open bank accounts, hire employees, and file for 501(c)(3) tax exempt status. An EIN is like a social security number for businesses. Actually it is misnamed because you do not need to be an employer to obtain an EIN. They are offered for free by the IRS. Go to www.irs.gov/taxtopics/tc755.html for more information on EINs.

Record some ideas for your legal name here:

_____

_____

_____

Picking a name

If for no other reason, your homeschool co-op needs a name so your family can call it *something*. A title will also let the homeschooling community know you exist! There are all kinds of names to chose from. Biblical names and themes are popular for faith-based co-ops such as Koinonia, which means fellowship, or Veritas, which means truth. Other examples include Wisdom's Gate, Agape, Alpha, and Lighthouse. Acronyms also work well. Here are some:

- Parents Offering Inspiration, Nurturing, and Training (POINT)
- Creative Home Educators Support Services (CHESS)
- Higher Extension Learning Program (HELP)
- Homeschool Eclectic Lifelong Learners Organization (HELLO)
- Life-long Education And Discipleship (LEAD)

- Home Educators Applying Righteous Teaching (HEART)
- Home Oriented Unique Schooling Experience (HOUSE)
- Life Education And Resource Network (LEARN)

As an alternative to an acronym, many homeschool co-ops prefer to use the name of their town in their name. My co-op is called the Mason Home School Co-op. This type of name is distinct and simple to identify. Some groups do not use the word "co-op", so they might call themselves Tuesday Group, Leaves of Learning, Learning Tree or New Horizons. Also phrases such as "Extension Program" and "Resource Center." are popular. One group named Providence Extension Program, goes by the affectionate acronym PEP.

Brainstorm some acronyms or other names here:

_____

_____

_____

Not a school

I recommend that you avoid any word that would confuse your co-op with a school. Often, I see the word "academy" or "school" used in names of homeschool co-ops. These terms name might imply that you are a full service school. Homeschool co-ops are not schools because schools have a lot of regulations that homeschool co-ops do not need to follow. In choosing your name, do not pick anything that might confuse your potential members or the homeschooling community at large.

Not already taken

You need to make sure your name has not already used by another organization. Typically, using your city and state name in your legal title helps to avoid duplication. If you decide to become an IRS-recognized charity you will need to do a name search to be sure your name is not already taken. Visit your Secretary of State's website. Most states offer name searches for free. Also, you can visit the IRS's tax exempt web site (www.irs.gov/eo) and do a name search there.

Defining Your Mission

Mission statements are a concise way to state your organization's purpose. They help focus and clarify the goal of your organization. Mission statements must tell others who you are and remind your leaders and members of your focus.

Who and Why

A mission statement answers two questions:

Who are you? Are you defined geographically, by religious affiliation, by age of students, by skills, styles or by curriculum choice? Who is your target audience? Do you want to attract parents, kids, athletic students, musical students, high school students, etc?

Why do you exist? Is it to encourage parents, support students, offer information, conduct classes, promote homeschooling or provide field trips?

Write down your WHO answers here:

_____

_____

_____

Record your WHY answers:

_____

_____

_____

Although a mission statement should explain who and why you exist, it does not include how you will accomplish your purpose. The answer to this question would be a general summary of what programs your co-op will provide such as holding classes, running a sports program, organizing field trips, etc. The detailed description of your activities should be in another statement called a Program Statement.

Tips for Writing a Mission Statement

- Use words like try, seek, influence and encourage.

- Keep your mission statement short, ideally one sentence or about 50 words.

- Be accurate. Do not make your purpose unattainable or sound loftier than you can accomplish. Your organization cannot be all things to all people.

- Put your mission statement everywhere. Include it on letterhead, posters and on a sign at every board meeting.

Sample Mission Statements

Here are some mission statements from homeschool co-ops that may give you inspiration:

- *The purpose of this organization shall be to provide support, information and encouragement to homeschooling families.*

- *This group exists to teach and disseminate educational materials to parents of homeschooled children.*

- *The mission of this homeschool co-op is to provide affordable, quality, fun-filled academic classes to children in the homeschool community.*

- *We exist to encourage, support and build up a community of Christian homeschool families.*

Brainstorm a few mission statements here:

_____

_____

_____

_____

_____

_____

Limiting Your Purpose

You can't please all of the people all of the time

-John Lydgate

As I have said before, a single homeschool group cannot be all things to all people. The previous sections about defining your group's mission and purpose are to help you focus and limit your mission. This is a healthy practice. By limiting your group's scope, you can better focus on the people you will serve. One leader of my local homeschool co-op, Laura Cripe, put it best when she said, "I know we can't be everything to everyone. If you don't fit our group or our group doesn't fit you, we will help you find a group that does."

Perhaps the best way to focus your purpose is to list all the things your group will *not* be. This exercise is not meant to be exclusionary, but to simply help you define your area of emphasis. Some co-ops have a family focus and cover all ages, while others naturally limit themselves to a geographic region. Still others focus on a particular area such as academics, science, or literature. At the other end of the spectrum, some co-ops are non-academic and offer the fine arts or extra curricular subjects. Also some homeschool groups use parents as volunteer teachers, while others hire paid teachers.

Make a list of what your group will *not* be:

_____

_____

_____

Consider this list of items in determining your group's focus and purpose:

- Age of students
- Geographic location
- Academic or enrichment focus
- Subject-specific (such as a science or literature)
- Parent or teacher led
- Focus on support for the parent
- Emphasis on classroom instruction
- Offer field trips or other programs
- Low cost or "market" price

- Inclusive (encompassing all faiths and backgrounds)
- Like-minded (shared faith or belief)

One group's story of choosing a mission

Linda Jordan from New Hampshire writes in Home Education magazine about how her homeschool group (called the Homeschool Resource Center) chose a mission statement. Note how she states her "Who" and "Why" issues and also indirectly addressed what they are *not*.

We had started out as a loosely knit group of mothers who just wanted to get together and provide some social life for ourselves, our children and other local homeschooling families, to create a kind of once-a-week neighborhood where our kids could play together and we could just hang out, chat, vent and seek advice. By halfway through the first year, it became apparent that we needed to meet regularly outside resource center hours to plan and to resolve issues that inevitably arose.

It also became apparent that we needed to put our vision into words, in order to explain it to others and to evaluate how other people's ideas might fit in. What we came up with was this: 'Our vision is to create a space for families to gather where all feel included, a place where children are free to decide for themselves what activities they will be involved in; and to encourage development of a homeschooling community.'

We have revisited this statement numerous times in response to specific requests or issues, and so far haven't felt a need to modify it. We actively embrace the idea of 'perpetual recess,' because we feel that's what is most lacking in our home school experience. In southern New Hampshire, children have ample opportunity to participate in classes and field trips, but it's very hard to find time for them to just hang out with other kids and do kid stuff.[16]

Linda saw a need in her homeschooling community for a place to "just hang out." She and the other leaders incorporated that purpose in their mission statement. They obviously put some time and thought into their particular group's focus. They didn't even try to be all things to all people.

Identifying Who You Are by Writing Bylaws

The pinnacle of determining your group's purpose and focus will be by creating bylaws. Bylaws spell out how the organization will operate and configure the board of directors. They also state the organization's rules of internal operation. For example, the bylaws specify the number of members of the board, the length of time each member serves on the board, the officer positions, and how meetings are conducted. Some states require bylaws, especially if your organization plans to incorporate as a nonprofit corporation.

One of the first duties of the board of directors is to write and approve the bylaws. A ten-year-old homeschool group in North Carolina benefited from creating bylaws right from the start:

When I [Beth H.] started our group 10 years ago with two friends, we sat down and decided on a purpose statement and wrote bylaws, based on what our vision was for the support group that was yet to be. For instance, we decided that ours would be a Christian support group that required a statement of faith. We decided that we would not put a cap on the number of families we would accept. We decided that we would have a seven member board of directors (okay, there were only three of us, but this is what we were working toward!) and that board members would have two-year terms and be voted on by the membership. For our purpose, we stated that our group was meant to encourage and support Christian home school families in our area; that we would work together to provide social, academic, and character-building activities for our children; and that we would share information of interest to homeschooling families.

That first year, we had almost 20 families. One mom started a 4-H group, we had PE [Physical Education] days at the park, we had oral presentation days each month, we had a mom's meeting one night a month, and we planned a few field trips. The following year we added a Thursday afternoon co-op for eight weeks in the fall and eight weeks in the spring. Activities came and went as parents stepped forward to plan and lead. That group has now grown to 250 families. Having written guidelines in place from the very beginning has helped as we have grown, because everyone knew up front what our purpose was, how we were structured, and how things operated.[17]

This group got off to a great start because they focused on their mission very early and wrote bylaws. They were obviously very successful by growing from 20 to 250 families. The bylaws should not be changed frequently, but should allow for the flexibility of programs as Beth mentioned.

What to Include in Your Bylaws

- Name: the legal name of your organization, not the "Doing Business As" name.

- Purpose: Be very specific. Use a mission statement or a Bible verse if desired.

- Location: city, county and state.

- Qualifications of members: Not all homeschool organizations have official members. Some groups do not have membership requirements and let everyone come to their events. Members do not have to be given the right to vote. Sometimes it is cumbersome to get members together for a meeting or a vote. If you do decide to have requirements for joining consider these qualifications for membership:

  - Payment of dues

  - Agreement with a statement of faith

- Requirement to be legally homeschooling according to state laws (As opposed to just "homeschooling" or even just "interested in homeschooling")

- Membership in a state or national group

- Membership in a particular church denomination (i.e. Catholic) or religious faith (i.e. Jewish)

• Meetings: How often will the board meet? Is a quorum required? Is a majority vote required? Will proxy votes be allowed? How will the meetings be announced and scheduled?

• Board of Directors and Officers. Consider the following issues:

- Will the board be elected by members or be self-elected? Will the terms be one year or more? Will there be a maximum term of service to the board? Many boards set a limit of three years of service and one year off the board before serving again. This prevents an extremely long term without change of leadership. I recommend that an officer serve no longer than three years at a time.

- What are the position descriptions for president, vice president, treasurer and secretary?

- What are the qualifications of board members? Should they be a general member of the group for at least a year before serving on the board?

- Can a married couple both serve?

• Committees: How are committees formed? ("At the request of the Board" is usually a good idea.)

• Tax exempt provisions: Include the following words from the IRS if your organization will be filing for 501(c)(3) tax exempt status (See Chapter Ten "The Next Step: 501(c)(3) Tax Exempt Status"):

a. *Upon the dissolution of _____, assets shall be distributed for one or more exempt purposes within the meaning of section 501(c)(3) of the Internal Revenue Code, or corresponding section of any future federal tax code, or shall be distributed to*

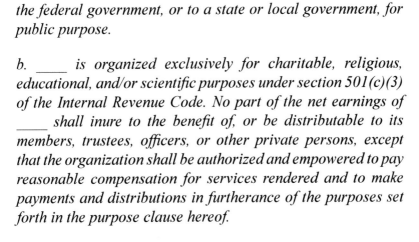

the federal government, or to a state or local government, for public purpose.

b. _____ is organized exclusively for charitable, religious, educational, and/or scientific purposes under section 501(c)(3) of the Internal Revenue Code. No part of the net earnings of _____ shall inure to the benefit of, or be distributable to its members, trustees, officers, or other private persons, except that the organization shall be authorized and empowered to pay reasonable compensation for services rendered and to make payments and distributions in furtherance of the purposes set forth in the purpose clause hereof.

c. No substantial part of the activities of _____ shall be the carrying on of propaganda, or otherwise attempting to influence legislation, and the organization shall not participate in, or intervene in (including the publishing or distribution of statements) any political campaign on behalf of any candidate for public office.

d. Notwithstanding any other provision of this document, the organization shall not carry on any other activities not permitted to be carried on (a) by an organization exempt from federal income tax under section 501(c)(3) of the Internal Revenue Code, or corresponding section of any future federal tax code, or (b) by an organization, contributions to which are deductible under section 170(c)(2) of the Internal Revenue Code, or corresponding section of any future federal tax code.

What to Leave Out of Bylaws

Your bylaws should *not* include day-to-day operating policies such as:

- Dress codes
- Discipline policies
- Schedules

- Names of officers

- Start and end times

- Specific location or meeting place

Put these items in another document called a policy manual. Policy manuals are discussed in Chapter Six "Leadership."

Sample Bylaws

As you create your own bylaws, look at sample bylaws of other non-profit organizations. Many homeschool groups have put their bylaws online which can easily be found by doing an internet search on "homeschool bylaws." Following is a sample set of bylaws that I created by looking at several homeschool groups' bylaws. It is available electronically in Microsoft Word format at my website http://www.homeschoolcpa.com/. Feel free to edit it as your group sees fit.

Sample Bylaws for a Homeschool Co-op

Article 1 – Name, Purpose, Location

Section 1 – The name of this organization shall be _____.

Section 2 – _____ is organized exclusively for educational purposes. The mission of _____ is _____
_____.

Section 3 – The principle office location of _____ shall be located in _____ County in the State of _____ . The organization may have any number of offices at such places as the Board may determine.

Article 2 – Membership

Section 1 – The qualifications for membership in this organization are:
_____.

Section 2 – Membership to the organization is fee-based, requiring dues.

(Optional) Section 3 – Members of the organization shall have the right to one vote on matters submitted to a vote of the membership including election of officers.

Article 3 – Meetings

Section 1 – The date of the regular annual meeting shall be determined by the Board of Directors who will also set the time and place.

Section 2 – Regular meetings of the Board may be held at such place and time as shall be designated by the standing resolution of the Board.

Section 3 – Special meetings may be called by _____ (*Whom? the Chair or the officers?*).

Section 4 – Notice of all meetings shall be provided to each voting member, by _____(*mail, fax, email)* at least ____ weeks/days prior to the meeting.

Article 4 – Board of Directors

Section 1 – The business of the organization shall be managed by a Board of Directors comprised of at least ____ and no fewer than ____ Board members. The Board is responsible for maintaining the overall policy and direction of the organization. The Board shall delegate responsibility of day-to-day operations to the Executive Director and appropriate committees. Board members shall receive no compensation (other than reasonable expenses) for their service on the Board.

Section 2 – The Board shall meet at least ____ times per year at an agreed upon time and location. Board members shall not miss more than ____ meeting(s) per year.

Section 3 – All Board members shall serve for ____ year terms (staggered terms are optional) and can be eligible for re-election _____ times.

Section 4 – Any Director may be removed from office without assigning any cause by the vote of the Board at any meeting of the Board.

Section 5 – Any Director may resign at any time by giving notice to the organization.

Section 6 – In the event of a vacancy on the Board (including situations where the number of Board members has been deemed necessary to increase), the directors shall fill the vacancy.

Section 7 – A quorum must be attended by at least _____ percent of the Board members before business can be transacted or motions made or passed.

Article 5 – Officers

Section 1 – The officers of the organization shall be _____, _____, _____, _____. (*Titles of Chair or President, Secretary, Treasurer, not specific individual names*) The Board of Directors shall appoint each of these officers. The Board may also appoint other officers it deems necessary.

Section 2 – The Board of Directors shall appoint officers for a term established by the Board.

Section 3 – Any officer may be removed from office without assigning any cause by the vote of the Board at any meeting of the Board.

Section 4 – Officers of the Board will not be compensated via salary for their service as an officer of the Board.

Section 5 – Board Chair/President

The Chair shall convene regularly scheduled Board meetings and shall preside or arrange for other Directors to preside at each meeting in the following order: Vice Chair, Secretary and Treasurer. The Board Chair appoints Committee Chairs.

Section 6 – Vice Chair

The Vice Chair will chair committees on special subjects as designated by the board. In addition, the Vice Chair will facilitate meetings in the absence of the Board Chair.

Section 7 – Secretary

The Secretary shall be responsible for keeping records of Board actions, including overseeing the taking of minutes at all board meetings, sending out meeting announcements, distributing copies of minutes and the agenda to each Board member, and assuring that corporate records are maintained.

Section 8 – Treasurer

The Treasurer shall make a report at each Board meeting. The treasurer shall assist in the preparation of the budget, help develop fund raising plans, and make financial information available to Board members and the public.

Article 6 – Committees

Section 1 – The Board may create committees as needed, such as fund raising, membership, and program committees. The Board Chair shall appoint all committee chairs.

Section 2 – No committee shall have any power to: fill vacancies on the Board, adopt, amend or repeal the bylaws, amend or repeal any resolution of the Board, or act on matters committed by the bylaws or resolution of the Board to another committee of the Board.

Article 7 - IRC 501(c)(3) Tax Exemption Provisions

a. Upon the dissolution of _____, assets shall be distributed for one or more exempt purposes within the meaning of section 501(c)(3) of the Internal Revenue Code, or corresponding section of any future federal tax code, or shall be distributed to the federal government, or to a state or local government, for public purpose.

b. _____ is organized exclusively for charitable, religious, educational, and/or scientific purposes under section 501(c)(3) of the Internal Revenue Code. No part of the net earnings of _____ shall inure to the benefit of, or be distributable to its members, trustees, officers, or other private persons, except that the organization shall be authorized and empowered to pay reasonable compensation for services rendered and to make payments and distributions in furtherance of the purposes set forth in the purpose clause hereof.

c. No substantial part of the activities of _____ shall be the carrying on of propaganda, or otherwise attempting to influence legislation, and the organization shall not participate in, or intervene in (including the publishing or distribution of statements) any political campaign on behalf of any candidate for public office.

d. Notwithstanding any other provision of this document, the organization shall not carry on any other activities not permitted to be carried on (a) by an organization exempt from federal income tax under section 501(c)(3) of the Internal Revenue Code, or corresponding section of any future federal tax code, or (b) by an organization, contributions to which are deductible under section 170(c)(2) of the Internal Revenue Code, or corresponding section of any future federal tax code.

Article 8 – Amendments

Section 1 – These Bylaws may be amended when deemed necessary by a _____ majority vote of the Board of Directors. Proposed amendments must be submitted to____(*Whom? Secretary, Board Chair*)_____ and sent along with regular board meeting notices.

Part Two

Running a Homeschool Co-op

Chapter Six:
Leadership

Why You Can't Do This Alone

Quite simply, you cannot start and run a homeschool co-op by yourself. A homeschool mother, who had started a group all by herself, recently commented, "I've had some members suggest that we create a board of directors so that all responsibilities don't fall on me. Some of them are concerned that I will 'burn out.' How I start something like that?" I have summarized some of the advice she received about leader burn out and forming a board of directors:

- It is not only important but also necessary that you surround yourself with like-minded people.

- Leaders have to leave for many reasons besides burn-out: they move away; their children graduate; sometimes they or a family member fall ill or they may need to care for elderly parents. You should have a team in place to replace a leader for any of these reasons.

- If you have several people in leadership your group won't dissolve even if the person in charge has to step down for some reason. Also, continually raising up new leaders among your members ensures smooth succession.

- We have had a leadership team for many years. The workload is shared among three to five people. No one wants the sole responsibility for all the decision-making that goes on in a homeschool co-op.

This is all excellent advice from other homeschool leaders. I found that sharing leadership is encouraged in the Bible. We have the biblical example of Moses, who could not handle the burden of leadership alone. Some of you may be able to relate to how Moses felt when he complained to God:

> *He asked the LORD, 'Why have you brought this trouble on your servant? What have I done to displease you that you put the burden of all these people on me? ... I cannot carry all these people by myself; the burden is too heavy for me.'* (Numbers 11:11, 14)

In response, God directed Moses to:

> *'Bring me seventy of Israel's elders who are known to you as leaders and officials among the people.... They will help you carry the burden of the people so that you will not have to carry it alone.'* (Numbers 11:16,17)

Moses was feeling burned out, exhausted and frustrated. In the book of Exodus, his father-in-law, Jethro, found Moses taking on too much of the load.

> *The next day Moses took his seat to serve as judge for the people, and they stood around him from morning till evening. When his father-in-law saw all that Moses was doing for the people, he said, 'What is this you are doing for the people? Why do you alone sit as judge, while all these people stand around you from morning till evening?'*

*Moses answered him, 'Because the people come to me to seek
God's will. Whenever they have a dispute, it is brought to me,
and I decide between the parties and inform them of God's
decrees and laws.'*

*Moses' father-in-law replied, 'What you are doing is not good.
You and these people who come to you will only wear yourselves
out. The work is too heavy for you; you cannot handle it alone.
Listen now to me and I will give you some advice, and may God
be with you. You must be the people's representative before
God and bring their disputes to him. Teach them the decrees
and laws, and show them the way to live and the duties they are
to perform. But select capable men from all the people—men
who fear God, trustworthy men who hate dishonest gain—and
appoint them as officials over thousands, hundreds, fifties and
tens. Have them serve as judges for the people at all times, but
have them bring every difficult case to you; the simple cases
they can decide themselves. That will make your load lighter,
because they will share it with you. If you do this and God so
commands, you will be able to stand the strain, and all these
people will go home satisfied.' Moses listened to his father-in-
law and did everything he said.* (Exodus 18:13-27)

Does this situation sound like you and your homeschool group? When
there is a problem, are you the "answer woman" (or man)? If you find
yourself exhausted and overwhelmed, follow Jethro's advice and pick
some others to help carry the burden. Many blessings will come when
you follow this advice. One homeschool leader put Jethro's advice into
practice. She worked for a year to train a replacement so she would not
burn out from exhaustion.

Basically, the idea is that she [the replacement leader] will be
walking side by side with me throughout the year, attending all
planning meetings, being a secondary contact for questions.
She will also assume some duties that will help familiarize her
with the membership, i.e. assembling the membership roster
and emergency call lists, and assuming primary responsibility
in organizing our fall meeting. This will give her a year of

walking through the process and always knowing she has me to fall back on before assuming full leadership. After a couple years of me asking... 'doesn't someone else want to do this?' I thought this might be a way to ease someone into leadership without it seeming like such an overwhelming task.[18]

Choosing a Leadership Team

Ask personally

If after reading my exhortation in the preceding section, you feel you need support, how should you go about finding someone to help you? First, you should prayerfully look over your co-op membership roster for people with qualifications (see Qualifications for Leaders later in this chapter). Make up a list of tasks needing to be done and approach an experienced person. I recommend you contact a potential helper personally, by either calling or asking them face to face. Emphasize their strengths and contributions to your organization and ask if they would be willing to help in a leadership role.

Define the task

Keep tasks well defined and limited. Some people are reluctant to volunteer for leadership because they fear there is no getting out later! If you define a role specifically and limit the term (perhaps one year), the potential helper may commit freely. A few years ago my co-op found it difficult for the director to make morning announcements because she had so many other responsibilities at the start of co-op. After looking around, our board noticed that one particular woman was always there on time (or early), had a strong voice and had already assumed some leadership by organizing field trips. We asked her to take over the job of doing morning announcements for the next semester, complimenting her organizational skills and promptness! She agreed and lifted a weight from our director.

Form committees

Most homeschool co-ops keep their leadership teams small so decisions can be made easily. Every team should have at least three members: a president, a secretary and a treasurer. In addition, some groups prefer to add a vice president who will succeed the current president. As responsibilities increase, the size of the team should grow as well. Many groups like to add program, planning and membership duties to leadership team members.

Most co-op boards create committees which meet outside of regular meetings to handle many tasks. Committee members may not be regular board members. A co-op of twenty to one hundred families might have a leadership team of about four or five members and two to five committees. Some jobs can be performed by a committee of one person. My own co-op of 50 families has a leadership team of six people (chair, treasurer, secretary, and three other members) and at least 12 other people serving in specific volunteer jobs. (See Chapter Nine "Managing Volunteers.") One example of a committee doing an excellent job occurred when my co-op needed to find a new location. We formed a search committee of three people who worked for about three months together and found us a great church to host our Friday co-op.

Possible Committees for a Homeschool Co-op:

- Registration
- Building use
- Classes & teachers
- Events
- Hospitality
- Financial
- Fundraising
- Membership
- Welcoming new members

- Homeschooling information
- Field trips
- Legislative liaison

Can you think of more tasks or committees? Most likely there are several positions unique to your co-op. List them here, and then add a potential person to fill each role. As you make your list, pray and ask God to give you names.

_____

_____

_____

_____

Qualifications for Leaders

The nonprofit website, Board Source (**www.boardsource.com**), has a list of personal characteristics to consider for your leadership team or board:

- Able to listen, analyze, think clearly and creatively; to work well with people individually as well as in a group.

- Willing to prepare for and attend board and committee meetings, to ask questions, and to take responsibility and follow through on a given assignment.

- Possessing honesty; a friendly, responsive, and patient approach; community-building skills; personal integrity; a sense of values; a concern for your group's development; and a sense of humor.

Besides these, I would add "common sense" qualifications like these:

- Shows up on time and comes prepared to co-op
- Committed to the group and homeschooling
- Friendly and well-liked
- Mature and can make decisions
- Available. Do not lay more responsibilities on a mother already carrying a heavy load.

Duties of the Board of Directors

Your leadership team may also be called a board of directors, but whatever the name the responsibilities are common to all leaders of nonprofit organizations. The basic responsibilities of nonprofit boards include:

- Determining the organization's mission and purpose.
- Selecting the chief executive, sometimes called a Director or Leader in homeschooling groups.
- Providing proper financial oversight. The board must develop an annual budget and monitor spending during the year.
- Ensuring legal integrity and maintaining accountability. The board is responsible for knowing and following any legal standards, especially if the co-op is a 501(c)(3) tax exempt organization.
- Recruiting and welcoming new board members and evaluating their own performance as a board.
- Guarding the organization's reputation. The board should know the organization's mission, accomplishments, and goals.
- Supporting the organization's programs and services. The board's responsibility is to determine which programs are consistent with the organization's mission and to monitor their effectiveness. Basically, the board members pitch in where needed!

Legal Responsibilities of Boards

There are three legal responsibilities for leaders: the duty of care, the duty of loyalty and the duty of obedience.

Duty of Care

In legal jargon this means "care that an ordinarily prudent person would exercise in a like position and under similar circumstances." Essentially, a board member should exercise reasonable care when he or she makes a decision as a steward of the organization.

Duty of Loyalty

The duty of loyalty is a standard of faithfulness. A board member should never use information obtained as a member for personal gain, but instead must act in the best interests of the organization.

Duty of Obedience

The duty of obedience requires board members to be faithful to the organization's mission. They are not permitted to act in a way that is inconsistent with the central goals of the organization. It also means that the organization will manage their funds to fulfill the organization's mission.

I like the way that the Bellevue Home School Enrichment organization in Tennessee worded their constitution. You may also include these duties in your bylaws:

Article I: Responsibilities of the Board of Directors

Section I: The board shall be alert to the program's needs and problems, and promote and provide for good parent-teacher relations. It shall resolve problems that hinder a proper functioning of the program.

Section II: The board shall resolve any ongoing discipline problems or other unresolved problems.

Section III: The board shall approve classroom standards, policies, and procedures.[19]

Visit Bellevue's website at www.EnrichmentBHSE.com for their entire constitution with board duties for director, treasurer and secretary.

Membership Requirements

Determining who should belong to your group can become a sticky situation. As I declared in Chapters Four and Five, I will reemphasize that your group cannot be all things to all people. When you decide whom to allow to join your co-op, make up a list of membership requirements. Consider these requirements that I have collected from several home school organizations:

- Paying dues or fees
- Signing a statement of faith (see the statement of faith section below)
- Volunteering some predetermined amount of time (twice a year, one hour a week, etc. depending on your program)
- Homeschooling as it is legally defined in your state (see the following section)
- Agreeing to the group's policy statements which often include dress codes, conflict resolution guidelines and codes of conduct

Should we allow public school or charter school students?

Allowing public or charter school students into your homeschool co-op is certainly a hot topic in homeschooling right now. For years the lines between homeschooling and public schooling were pretty clear. Now, however, technology has allowed public-schooled children to be educated in their own homes. These programs might be called charter schools or virtual schools. Not all virtual schools are public school extensions; The Potter's School (www.pottersschool.org) is an good example of a virtual homeschool program. Charter or virtual public-schooled students *feel* as if they are homeschooled because they learn at home, not in their public school building. While they might call themselves homeschoolers, I prefer to think of them as "public school students learning at home," but that is a bit of a mouthful.

Ultimately, the question is whether public-schooled children should be allowed to join your homeschool co-op. This is not an easy decision, but some groups have decided to exclude charter/public-schooled students. While these groups have several reasons for their choice, most of their reasons have nothing to do with individual students or their families, but rather their motives involve the hard-fought rights of freedom in homeschooling. Since some homeschoolers feel very strongly that their rights and freedoms are being eroded by charter/public schools, they are taking an important stand for what they feel is right by excluding public-school students from homeschool organizations. One homeschool group wrote to their co-op members about their decision concerning charter/public-schooled students. Some portions are edited for brevity. See http://www.hslda.org/hs/state/oh/CharterCyberSchools.pdf for the entire letter.

> Dear Members of _____Homeschool Co-op,
>
> We firmly believe that each family has the right and responsibility to chose the educational format that will best serve their family, whether it be public, charter, private or home education.
>
> We do wish to be clear however that although students who are enrolled in Charter Cyber Schools are educated in their homes, this educational alternative differs from home education in significant ways.
>
> The _____Homeschool Co-op offers enrichment classes "designed to assist home school families by offering classes that support a Christ-centered world view..." Since we are established to support homeschoolers, we will offer classes only to families who are currently home educating their children.

Although this was undoubtedly a difficult decision, I admire this unnamed group for knowing their mission and fixing their focus on that mission. If you care to read more about this issue, you can read the *CHEO Position Paper on Cyber Community Schools* [20] at the Christian Home Educator of Ohio website (www.cheohome.org). Please note that CHEO is not taking a position on all cyber or virtual schools, but just those chartered as public schools in Ohio (called Community schools).

This issue will mostly likely confront you when your board is asked to admit a family that uses a charter/public school. A few years ago, this happened to my group. Some co-op members knew the charter/public-schooled family personally and wanted them in our co-op. The mother had chosen to use our state's virtual public school for financial reasons as the computer and curriculum were all provided free of charge. You can imagine her distress when she was told that she was "not really homeschooling" and could not join our co-op which requires members to be legally homeschooling in Ohio. Her children, however, were public school students learning at home. Those who knew her did their best to find another support group for her and kept in touch with her over the year. Eventually she stopped using the charter/public-school and returned to "true" homeschooling.

Statement of Faith

Needed or not?

Most Christian homeschool groups have a statement of faith in order to clearly spell out what co-op members believe. A written statement of faith establishes a common ground and a shared faith experience. As one member put it, "We are all like-minded in our desire to home educate and in our faith." In my co-op, members attend several different churches, yet we agree on the basic ideas in our statement of faith.

Some groups require all members to sign a statement of faith, which are usually broad in nature and concur with the beliefs of most church-going Christians. Some groups compose a statement of faith for the organization as a whole but require only that the member acknowledge the statement's existence; individual members are not asked to sign the statement of faith. Because members recognize the group's religious beliefs, members of these groups should not be surprised or offended if specific religious beliefs are introduced in co-op classes.

Other groups require only their leaders to sign the statement of faith, meaning the general membership does not have to agree on religious issues. This can work well for some people but not for others, depending on the expectation of each member. If they expected that a co-op teacher would not introduce alternative religious views, then they will not be comfortable in a "open membership" group.

The Eads family, a homeschooling family from Indiana, describes the importance of writing a statement of faith:

> When designing a statement of faith for your homeschool co-op, it is important to ask yourself what you are trying to accomplish by having a statement of faith. Many co-ops use a statement of faith as a tool to strengthen the group by having families of like minds and kindred hearts.
>
> By nature a statement of faith will do two things:
>
> 1) Remind those that will be in the group that our faith in Jesus is central to everything we do, especially teaching our children.
>
> 2) Exclude families that do not share the faith we have.
>
> It is important to say here that we do not exclude families because they are bad, or that we are better than them. We seek to exclude families that do not share a common kindred heart because we believe that teaching our children about Jesus is the most important thing a parent can do.[21]

The Eads have placed a tool on their website with several helpful guidelines and wording choices to help you build your own statement of faith. Because this tool is very detailed and specific, you can edit it and chose what suits your group best. Visit it at www.eadshome.com/statementfaith2.htm.

Sample Statements of Faith

An internet search of "homeschool statement of faith," generated 1,240,000 hits! Apparently, there is no shortage of sample statements out there to pick from. It seems every homeschool support group, co-op, magazine and vendor have a statement of faith. I have included only a few examples here to get you started.

This sample is from Desert Hills Christian Homeschoolers. The group, established in 1986, is the oldest homeschool support group in Arizona. Their statement of faith is short and clear:

- We believe the Bible is the Word of God; inspired and without error in its original manuscripts. It is our only source of authority in matters of faith, conduct, and truth.

- We believe there is one eternal God, personal and knowable, who manifests Himself in three distinct Persons: God the Father, God the Son, and God the Holy Spirit. He is worthy of our worship, confidence, and obedience.

- We believe in Jesus Christ, God's only begotten son, conceived by the Holy Spirit. We believe in His virgin birth, sinless life, miracles, teachings, substitutionary death, bodily resurrection, ascension into Heaven, perpetual intercession for His people, and personal visible return to earth.

- We believe the ministry of the Holy Spirit is to convict the lost of sin, righteousness and judgment; place and seal the believer in the Body of Christ, and make real the productive things of Christ in the believers life. We do not believe that any particular or special gift is necessary evidence of salvation or of being filled with the Holy Spirit; although we do believe in the gifting and exercise of all Biblical gifts of the Holy Spirit.

- We believe that every person is born with a sin nature, is spiritually dead and cannot please God until Christ gives him eternal life. We believe that salvation from sin, death and hell is by Gods grace. It must be received by faith apart from any human performance or merit. It is a free gift of God to anyone who personally places his confidence in the Lord Jesus and His finished work on the cross. We believe a truly born-again person is secure in Christ.[22]

The Homeschoolers of Wyoming (H.O.W.) require their board members to agree with this statement of faith, but not individuals wishing to participate in activities offered by H.O.W.

We Believe...

- The Bible is the inspired and infallible Word of God and constitutes His completed and final revelation to man. The Bible, in its original autograph, is without error in whole and in part, including theological concepts as well as geographical and historical details.

- God has existed from eternity in three persons: God the Father, God the Son, and God the Holy Spirit. Jesus Christ was God come in human flesh being fully God and fully man, except without sin.

- All men are in violation of God's righteous requirements and His holy character both by nature and act, and are therefore under His wrath and just condemnation.

- The central purpose of the coming of Jesus Christ was to pay the penalty for man's sin through His substitutionary death on the cross, the successful accomplishment of which was attested to by His subsequent visible, bodily resurrection.

- Salvation is offered as a gift, free to the sinner. This gift must be responded to in individual faith, not trusting in any personal works whatsoever, but in the sacrificial death of Jesus Christ alone.[23]

The shortest statement of faith I found was from the Helping Hands Co-op in central Texas.

We believe:

- The Bible is the inspired and only infallible and authoritative written Word of God.

- In the deity of our Lord Jesus Christ, God's only begotten Son, in His eternal pre-existence, in His virgin birth, in His sinless life, in His vicarious and atoning death, in His bodily resurrection, in His ascension to the right hand of the Father, where He reigns as King of kings and Lord of lords forever. (John 3:16, John 1:1-18, Ephesians 2:8)

- The only means of being cleansed from sin is through repentance and faith in the precious blood of Jesus Christ.[24]

These samples of statements of faith may serve as a launching point for your homeschool co-op. Writing a statement of faith should be done thoughtfully and carefully by the leadership board. Some co-ops also ask for input from the co-op members at large. Including everyone in this important document can build cohesion and a sense of community.

Writing a Policy Manual

After determining your group's mission and deciding the four Ws (What, Who, When and Where) from Chapter Four, the biggest job for your leaders will be to create and approve a policy manual. This very helpful document is the rulebook for your co-op. While, it is more detailed than bylaws, it can be easily changed as the need arises. The primary purpose of a policy manual is to avoid problems before they come up as well as give all co-op members guidelines on how to deal with problems. The policy manual is written when cool, impartial heads prevail, making a crisis or problem easier to cope with in a harmonious manner.

What to Put into Your Policy Manual

- Volunteer obligations
- Parent duties
- Student responsibilities

- Teacher requirements

- Money and payment policies (When should payments be due? Are there late fees?)

- Parent attendance or drop off policy

- Recess and lunch time rules (Can children play outside?)

- Clean up and building use (Some rented buildings do not allow food; others want only clear liquids.)

- Dress codes

- Student attendance and missed sessions

- Grading, homework and credits

- Behavior guidelines. (No running, no yelling, no punching, etc.)

- Sickness (when a child may not attend co-op because of illness, fever, rashes, etc.)

- Conflict resolution guidelines

Sample Policy Manuals

Although I will not reproduce Policy Manuals here, I will direct you to several examples from homeschool co-ops. Some co-ops try to set policies by example rather than specific rules. See the Standard of Conduct at http://eadshome.com/conduct.htm for an idea of general guidelines without specific rules.

Helping Hands Enrichment's policies:

http://webpages.charter.net/hmschlmomof3/index.htm

The Thursday Connection Co-op:

http://thursdayconnection.org/policies_and_procedures.htm.

Bellevue Home School Enrichment:

http://www.enrichmentbhse.com/ClassInfo.html

My own co-op has its Policy Manual on-line at http://www.masoncoop. org/3.html. It's quite lengthy at 10 pages.

Groups can live and die on leadership. Ensure the success of your homeschool co-op by carefully choosing a leadership team and helping your board member to be familiar with their duties and responsibilities. Likewise, your membership at large should know what is required of them. By establishing a written statement of faith and a policy manual your co-op leaders can build a solid foundation for a successful, healthy homeschool co-op.

Chapter Seven:
Co-op Offerings

This chapter is full of ideas gathered from dozens of homeschool co-ops from across the country. There are lists of classes by age, topic and curriculum. I list extracurricular activities that co-ops offer in addition to academic classes and even ideas for parent activities. This chapter should get your ideas flowing, so I have left room for you to jot down ideas of your own.

Classes Based on a Curriculum

Homeschoolers have a great variety of quality curricula to use, many of which can be easily adapted for teaching in a co-op. Please make sure you abide by the publishers' guidelines when using curriculum in a co-op class setting. Usually this means that each student must purchase his own textbook—no photocopying allowed!

- *The Mystery of History* by Linda L. Hobar for grades 5-8 (or 3-12 with modifications). Author Linda Hobar taught this curriculum at my homeschool co-op several times, so it is quite adaptable for a co-op.

- Mapping the World by Heart class for grades 7-12. Teach geography using the *Mapping the World by Heart* materials. Students learn to draw and label geography of countries, land, and water.

- *A History of Science* by Beautiful Feet for grades 5 and up. It includes basic science principles; the history of scientific study; and biographies of famous scientists like Archimedes, Galileo, and Einstein.

- Precepts for Kids for grades 4 to 6 using *Wrong Way, Jonah!; Jesus in the Spotlight; Jesus – Awesome Power, Awesome Love!; Jesus – To Eternity and Beyond!* all by Kay Arthur and Janna Arndt. Children observe, interpret, and apply God's Word.

- *Story of the World (Volumes I-IV)* by Susan Wise Bauer for grades 1-6. This curriculum includes discussion, map work, crafts, games, and science experiments.

- Great Science Adventures for grades 4 to 6 using the series by Dinah Zike including *Discovering the Human Body and Senses*, *World of Plants*, *World of Space*, etc.

- *Lord of the Rings* writing class for grades 8 and up using a course by Homescholar Books which includes literary analysis and interpretation and epic literature, including *The Iliad, The Odyssey, Beowulf,* and *The Aeneid.*

- *Institute for Excellence in Writing* for grades 4 and up: This is a writing curriculum concentrating on sentence structure and the use of grammar in selected literature, outlining models of literature and recreating paragraphs, and basic essay writing.

- Apologia Science books including *Exploring Creation with Astronomy,* etc. for elementary ages and Biology, Chemistry, Physics, etc. for high school students.

- *Tapestry of Grace* by Marcia Sommerville is a thorough history and literature program for all ages. The author also shares ideas for an end-of-year program to demonstrate what the students have learned.

- *Youth Exploration Survey (YES)* from Crown Financial Ministries. This is a career exploration curriculum that I have used several times in a co-op setting. It is best for 9th-12th grades.

Clubs in Co-op

Many homeschooling families love the idea of "one stop shopping" within their homeschool co-ops, meaning that all children's activities are on co-op day. This may means that clubs and other activities can be held during co-op hours. Following are some examples of clubs and activities that homeschool co-ops offer.

- Awana
- American Heritage Girls
- Keepers at Home
- Contenders
- 4-H
- Band/Music ensembles
- Bible Quiz
- Boy Scouts
- Junior Achievement
- Book Club
- Service Clubs

Classes by Age

In this section, I have compiled class ideas based on the age range of students. These lists are by no means complete as co-op teachers are very creative people and their ideas are endless.

For (Almost) All Ages

By saying "for all ages," I do not necessarily mean having all ages together in one class, although some brave homeschool co-op teachers have done that! Instead, I mean that with modifications these subjects can be taught to students from 5 to 18-year- olds. Most co-ops offer these classes every year; they are the "staple" of co-op offerings.

- Art
- Bible Study
- Choir/Singing
- Crafts
- Drama
- Dance
- Drawing
- Foreign Language especially Spanish
- Gym
- Music
- Science

Pre-School Ideas

- Art

- Bible Stories

- Gym

- Music

- Kindermoves: a class of games and musical activities including stretching and moving to songs and basics skills including throwing, jumping, running, batting etc.
- Adventure with Books: unit studies on storybooks with map work, art, cooking, and vocabulary that accompany each book.

Jot down some ideas you have for preschool classes:

_____

_____

_____

Kindergarten to Third Grade Ideas

- Signs for Little Fingers: basic sign language words commonly used in childhood ("please", "thank you", "drink"), animal names, colors, days of week, and simple nursery rhymes or songs

- Math Mania: math tasks (addition, subtraction, multiplication, division, measurements) using games

- Character First: teach character qualities using stories with songs, crafts and games

- Ancient History (or any period in history): map work, crafts, games and food of the world's oldest cultures

- Ballet Basics: basic ballet techniques, stretches, movements, short dances and games

- Me Gusta el Espanol (I Like Spanish): games, songs and role playing, along with vocabulary

- Exploring Words: pronunciation, spelling and meaning of new words, dictionary skills, and Greek and Latin roots

- Music Education: classical, jazz, folk, blues, patriotic, and well-loved songs we learned as children

- Gym: teamwork, sportsmanship and following directions

- A Trip Around the World: basic geographic and cultural features, facts, cooking and crafts

- American History: video or DVD selections, arts and crafts, and a sampling of foods

- Songbirds: foundation in music through learning and singing together

- US Presidents: memorizing the names of all presidents in chronological order

Hopefully these ideas have inspired you. Jot down some ideas you have for Kindergarten through third grade classes:

_____

_____

_____

Fourth to Sixth Grade Ideas

Many of these class ideas for 4th to 6th grade students can be offered in simplified form to younger students also. With modifications they can also be offered to older students in grades 7th and 8th.

- Drawing with Color: drawing with oil pastels, explore color theory, and good composition

- Cooking Around the World: make cuisine from countries from around the world

- Fencing: the sport and art of fencing

- Introduction to Spanish: listening, speaking, reading and writing in Spanish

- Ballroom Dance: different types of ballroom dance

- Micro Worlds: learn how a microscope works

- Jazz &Hip-Hop: the fun of jazz with stylized hip-hop street dance moves

- Literature: discuss books and study different writing styles

- Club Zoom: based on the PBS show "Zoom"; do science projects, games, activities, crafts

- Musical Theater: acting and singing, choreography, improvisation, vocal technique

- A History of Science (using *A History of Science* by Beautiful Feet): the history of scientific study including biographies of famous scientists

- Precepts for Kids (using *Wrong Way, Jonah!; Jesus in the Spotlight; Jesus – Awesome Power, Awesome Love!; Jesus – To Eternity and Beyond!* by Kay Arthur and Janna Arndt): Observe, interpret, and apply God's Word

- Cultures Through Arts & Crafts: designs and traditions found in the art and artifacts from the world's cultures

- Simple Literature: Short stories focusing on basic literary themes like the characters, setting and plot

- Discovering the Human Body (using the *Great Science Adventures*)

- Chemistry for Kids: introduction to basic chemical principles

- Music Education: listen to and learn about various styles of music, the biographies of famous musicians and the time periods of music

- Writing an Essay (using *Institute for Excellence in Writing*): sentence structure and the use of grammar, outlining, and basic essay writing.

- Latin I: read simple Latin passages, present, imperfect, and future verb tenses and learn vocabulary of about 125 words

- World Geography: fill in outline maps of all the continents, language, religion, art, music, missionary work, climate, animal and plant life and current events

- Physical Education: basketball; fitness walking; jogging; orienteering; rope jumping; soccer; softball; strength training; track & field; volleyball; and physical fitness testing/training

- Poetry: define and describe ten types of poetry, recognize and label rhyme/rhythm patterns

- Ancient Greece & Rome History and Literature (using Veritas Press): weekly writing and reading assignments

Does this list get your "juices" flowing? Record your ideas for 4th through 6th grade classes:

_____

_____

_____

_____

Seventh through Twelve Grade Ideas

Here's a mix of class ideas for older students, both academic and just plain fun in some cases.

- Jewelry: a basic class in jewelry making

- Lights! Camera! Acting!: games, improvisation and acting exercises

- Guitar: learn new songs and finger picking

- Mapping the World: geography using the *Mapping the World by Heart*

- Creative Writing: creative writing forms and literary devices

- Government: memorize parts of the Constitution and the Bill of Rights, and learn the history of the amendments

- Public Speaking: communication skills to speak in public

- Institute for Excellence in Writing: writing curriculum concentration on sentence structure, outlining, essay writing, critiques and research papers

- Bible Bowl: team competition of Bible questions

- *Exploring Creation with Physical Science*: basic matter, weather, physics of motion, Newton's laws, electricity and magnetism, light and sound

- Kids Kreations: basic cooking skills and kitchen safety; read and follow recipes; operate various kitchen appliances and equipment used in cooking.

- Conversational Spanish: learn Spanish in the context of dialogue

- Anatomy & Physiology: major systems of the human body; dissection of a frog, a fetal pig, and a cow's eye

- Advanced Public Speaking: speeches to give information, explain, encourage, and persuade

- Ancient History: ancient civilizations through the fall of the Roman Empire

- Ancient Literature: ancient literature including the *Epic of Gilgamesh*, Plato, Virgil and Homer

- SAT Prep: common math topics covered by the SAT

- Simply Desserts: preparing a variety of desserts including cakes, pies, pastries, and cookies

- Critical Thinking: activities, puzzles, games, reading

- Piano: private piano instruction

- *A Midsummer Night's Dream*: reading aloud and discussing the play and viewing a movie version.

If you need a few more ideas here is a list of classes offered by various homeschool co-ops for their junior and senior high school students. Let your imagination roam!

Accounting

Acrobic Excrcise

American History

Art Appreciation

Art History

Band

Basic Auto Mechanics

British Literature

Chess

Choir

Civil War History

Construction/Woodworking

Dance

Doll Making

Drama

Drawing

Election Process/Politics

Embroidery

Entrepreneurial Skills

First Aid

Great Composers

Latin

Logic

Mock Trial/Moot Court

Music Appreciation

Music History

Personal Finance

Photography

Puppets

Self Defense

Sign language

Stock Market Game

Voice

Wilderness survival training

This list is by no means complete! List your ideas for 7th through 12th grade classes here:

_____

_____

_____

_____

_____

Parent Class Ideas

Make sure parents are not left out of all the fun! Some co-ops offer classes for parents, too. Ideas include:

* Aerobics or walking group
* Bible Study
* Creative Writing
* Decorative Painting
* Family Genealogy
* Interior Decorating
* Investing Club
* Knitting, Crocheting

- Learning styles
- Personal Finances
- Photography
- Sewing

Make up your wish list below for adult offerings that interest you.

_____

_____

_____

_____

Classes by Topic Area

A wonderful, active co-op, the Homeschool Enrichment Program of Hays Hills Baptist Church in Texas[25], lists all the classes they have offered in the past. I have included their list by topic. There are neither detailed descriptions nor ages given, so you can let your imagination fly and just be inspired by the class titles. I like the titles "Boning up on Bones" and "Junior Librarian"!

Science & Nature:

Anatomy & Physiology

Bees, Bugs and Butterflies

Biology Lab

Body Science

Boning Up on Bones

Building Muscles

Creation Astronomy

Creation Science & Scripture

Earth Science

Flight & Rocketry

Habitats

Hands-on Science

Intro to Engineering Design

Intro to Physics

Introduction to Electronics

K'nex Levers & Pulleys

Microbiology

Nature Study

Nature Study & Sketching

Ocean Animals

Outdoor Activities

Phantastic Physics

Science Experiments

Science with Magic School Bus

Science with Picture Books

Seven Days of Creation

Solar System

History & Geography:

Ancient Egypt

Baseball/Softball History

Big Kid Blast

Bill of Rights/Declaration of Independence

Civics

Colonial Kids

Government

Hands-on History

I Love America

It's a Small World

Kids Learn America

Kings & Queens

Kings & Queens of England

Map Skills

More Than Moccasins

Russia

States & Capitals

Story of the World

Texas History & Geography

Trip Around the World

US Presidents

US States & Capitals

USA Geography

What About Sailing Ships

World Geography

Your Story Hour

Language Arts &Foreign Language:

Aesop's Puppets

American Sign Language

Beginning Spanish

Book About Me

Book Visions

C.S. Lewis

Could I Be a Poet?

Expository Writing Workshop

Grammar for Boys & Girls

Intro to German

Junior Librarian

Latin Enrichment

Mark Twain

Read & Learn

Sign Language Performance

Spanish I

Spanish II

Speed Reading & Writing

Spelling Mania

Stories and More

The Great Gatsby

The Lion, the Witch & the Wardrobe

The Lord of the Rings

Writing Creatively

Fine Arts, Drama, Oration & Music:

Acting

Character Development

Creative Movement

Drama

Dramatic Play

Ethics/Debate

Handbells

International Art & Culture

Masterpieces

Music

My Favorite Books

Oration

Public Speaking

Puppet Drama

Shakespeare

Six Artists and Their Work

Square Dancing

Start with a Song

Storytime

Twist and Shout

Art, Crafts & Hobbies:

Adventures in Art

Animal Art

Appreciating Art

Art with Different Media

Basic Guitar

Bible Crafts

Chess Club

Crafts

Crochet

Cut and Create Holidays

Decorative Painting

History & Making of American Samplers

How to Make Greeting Cards

Puppets

Scrapbooking

Sewing I

Super Cool Art

Upside Down Doll

Math & Economics

Curious Math

Economics & You

Finances for Kids

Game of Life

Life Skills for Kids

Money for Real Life

Thinking Critically About Advertising

Times Tables

Cooking

Beginning Cooking

Book-n-Cook

Creative Cakes

Delectable Desserts

Gobble Up the Bible

Make & Bake with Little House

More Than Soup

Pizza! Pizza!

Simply Home Cookin'

Vegetarian Cooking

Physical Education & Other Classes

An Old-Fashioned English Tea

Basketball/Football

Beginning Basics of Soccer & Basketball

Bootcamp Physical Training

Cardio & Conditioning

Charm & Poise for Girls

Computer Design & Layout

Hive of Busy Bees

Jump Rope Games

Mini Mysteries

Oops! Your Manners Are Showing

Physical Education

Presidential Champions

Princess & the Kiss

Where Are My Manners

Yearbook

Young Peacemaker

Additional Activities

Many co-op members are very creative when it comes to organizing co-op activities. Niki, a homeschool leader, shares how she organized an art show:

I sent out a flyer at the beginning of the year so the kids had plenty of time to save their artwork. I did create some categories such as crayon, pencil, chalk, collage, sculpture, etc. We also had a challenge self-portrait. All was judged by age. The art was displayed around the room. We also did some mini art class for the kids to get them excited about art. One was looking at artists, another for the older kids was trying to create a sculpture like Henri Moore, and the younger did paint splats outside with ketchup bottles and big smocks. The art is collected the day before and judged the day before. So that when they come it is already judged and they can go see their ribbons, enjoy others' art, and the mini-classes.[26]

Ideas for co-op activities are endless, but here are some ideas that others have tried:

- Culture Festival

- Drama Production

- Field Trips

- Geography Bee

- Graduation Banquet

- Graduation Ceremony

- Honor Society

- Open House

- Read a Mile

- Science Fair

- Spelling Bee

- Talent Show

- Used Book Sale

Service Projects

- Linus Project (Blankets)

- Prayer Shawl Ministry
- Nursing home visits
- Bibles for China
- Sponsor a child
- Letters to service men and women
- Valentines to shut-ins

Add to this list some activities your co-op might be interested in hosting:

_____

_____

_____

_____

I hope this chapter has given you some ideas of classes and activities that your homeschool co-op could undertake. Don't feel overwhelmed because no co-op does everything. Pick and chose what your students, families and volunteer teachers find most interesting. Remember that learning takes a lifetime!

Chapter Eight:
Money Management

Suppose one of you wants to build a tower. Will he not first sit down and estimate the cost to see if he has enough money to complete it? –Luke 14:28

While managing the money in a homeschool co-op can be challenging, every group needs to be fiscally responsible for the funds entrusted to them. A co-op should appoint a treasurer and keep a separate checking account. If your co-op is a medium or large group, the financial responsibilities become increasingly more demanding. These larger co-ops should establish a budget, keep good financial records, and have a treasurer give regular financial reports to leaders.

Small group management

When your homeschool group is very small, managing the funds can be quite easy. Many small groups do not open a separate checking account, but simply use cash to pay expenses. Since the dollar amounts are small (usually under $100), there is a level of trust. The leader could not embezzle much money, because there is not a lot to steal! No one expects a co-op leader to be guilty of theft, but temptations do occur. It is best not to mingle funds because the leader could easily "borrow" funds from the co-op on a week she is short on cash. Although she might not even consider it theft, it is.

Cash Basis

Some small groups operate on a cash basis. They collect cash only, no checks, from members for shared expenses like park fees or supplies. The unspent cash is kept in a safe place, like an envelope labeled "Homeschool Co-op Cash." My neighborhood has a flower fund that operates this way. About once a year, the organizer collects $5-$10 from each family. She simply drops a note in our mailboxes explaining that she will send flowers and cards to anyone in the neighborhood with a death or birth in the family. Because the dollar amounts are so small, there is no accountability or record keeping. We trust this lady who is volunteering out of the kindness of her heart. Unfortunately, with inflation causing prices to continually increase, $5 does not go very far anymore. You may find your group out grows its "cash only" system very quickly. If that is the case, I recommend that you open a separate checking account for your group.

Separate Checking Accounts

Once a homeschool organization has grown to about five or more families they may incur expenses like postage, printing, materials, and even rent. At this point, I would recommend a separate checking account. Sometimes, a treasurer will open a personal checking account rather than a business account to save on bank fees. I do not recommend this. If the treasurer has a personal account for handling the homeschool co-op's business, the cash in it could be seen as her *personal* income in the eyes of the IRS. I am sure she does not want that! Also, opening a personal checking account if there truly is an organization in operation is a bit untruthful to the bank.

Most banks offer free checking accounts to nonprofit organizations. When you open a nonprofit checking account your bank may ask for your organization's "Employer Tax Number" (or they many call it a "Tax ID number" or even an "IRS number.") Officially however, it is called an Employer Identification Number (EIN). This number is similar to a Social Security Number except it is for a business or organization. Even though your organization may have no employees and no business with the IRS, you need to get IRS Form SS-4 to obtain an EIN.

Tips for Getting an EIN from the IRS

To get an EIN, go to the IRS website (www.irs.gov) and search for "EIN." You can fill in the SS-4 online and receive an EIN within minutes, or you can print out the SS-4 and mail it in. Applications by mail can take weeks. A word of advice: under "Reason for applying," check the box "Banking purpose" and fill in the blank with "opening checking account." Another tip I have learned is to check "Other Nonprofit Organization" under "Type of Entity," and put "Educational Organization" in the blank. Finally, choose your name very carefully! (See Chapter Five "What's in a Name?")

Medium group management

As a homeschool co-op grows from small- to medium-sized, there are more financial duties. A medium-sized homeschool co-op might have five to twenty families. Usually, the group has survived its first year and is ready to continue into the future. The amounts of incoming cash as well as expenses add up quickly. While increased record keeping is needed, it should be kept simple. A medium home school group should:

- Open a separate checking account for non-profits, if not already done so.
- Appoint a treasurer.
- Establish a budget at the start of every year.
- Establish a simple record keeping system.

Open a Separate Checking Account

Keep the following recommendations in mind when opening a checking account:

- I *strongly* recommend purchasing duplicate checks. I know of a homeschool co-op that did not have duplicate checks. Because the treasurer was overwhelmed with other matters, she did not record the checks in the ledger. When the group wanted to create accurate financial statements, the treasurer did not know where the canceled checks were kept. The bank wanted to charge $5 *per check* to recreate copies from their system! Avoid this predicament by using duplicate checks.

- Use checks in numerical order. Do not rip off a check from the top of the next book because you will never know if checks are missing, forged, lost in the mail or written but never cashed.

- Have the bank account statements mailed to someone other than the treasurer. The co-op director would be a good choice. This is another person that is seeing what the checking account balance is every month.

- Choose a bank that allows online checking which makes downloading transactions very easy. With this service there is no need to type in every check or ATM transaction.

- Apply for a debit card, but give it only to responsible people who will not mix personal and co-op expenses. Those entrusted with the co-op's debit card must be careful to make only purchases allowed for in the budget.

- Never allow the treasurer to write checks to him/herself. Instead someone else with check signing privileges (perhaps the co-op's director) should make out any checks to the treasurer. This standard protects the reputation of the treasurer.

- Reconcile the checking account *every* month. Furthermore, the treasurer should be required to give a reconciliation report to the board on a regular basis.

Many medium-sized homeschool co-ops can use their check book ledger to create their financial statements. Does the director want to know how much money came in? Just add up deposits. If she wants to know how much profit the group has, then she can simply look at the checking account balance. This is a beautifully simple system *if* your keep your checking account up to date! On the other hand, if the co-op director asks questions like, "What did we spend on office supplies this year compared to last year?" your record keeping will have to be a little more sophisticated. The treasurer will actually have to do a bit of bookkeeping.

Appoint a Treasurer

Record keeping in mid-sized homeschool co-ops work best when the workload is shared. In a small group, the director or founder frequently handles the finances. As a co-op grows, however, the financial responsibility should be shared between a treasurer and the director. There are several reasons to appoint a treasurer:

- To divide the labor. Many hands make light work.

- To avoid mistakes. If the treasurer makes a mistake, then the director may spot it.

- To avoid fraud. We don't like to admit that it might happen, but sometimes even God-fearing people embezzle money. I read of a scout leader who skimmed money from the troop account for personal use. Unfortunately, it can happen in homeschool groups also. The list of recommendations for checking accounts (above) is some protection against fraud. Appointing a treasurer is another good defense against theft. Treasurers should also serve a predetermined term of at most three years, ensuring that a new person will look over the finances.

When you appoint a treasurer, look for a candidate with the following qualities:

- Honesty and integrity

- Good head for numbers

- Ability to balance a checking account
- Skills in how to create a spreadsheet or
- Knowledge of financial software like Microsoft Money or Quicken
- Analytical and precise thinking
- Organizational skills

Establish a Budget

In addition to appointing a treasurer to handle the co-op's finances, a medium-sized group should also establish a budget. Does the word "budget" sound like the word "diet" to you? It does to many people. While they may see a budget as a restraint, killjoy or taskmaster, it is really just a plan of how to allocate your money before you spend it. In personal finance, the word "budget" is frequently called a "spending plan." Your homeschool co-op should have a spending plan at the start of every year. This next section will show you how to get started planning your budget.

Preparing a Budget

Start Early

Ideally, your organization should prepare a budget before your program year starts. Although some people think that budgets track only spending, they must also include a plan for income. Start by listing all the sources of revenue you can think of (dues, class fees, fund-raisers, etc). Do not be too optimistic, as conservative estimates will serve you better than unrealistic goals.

Predict expenses

Next, try to predict expenses such as postage, copying, insurance, building use fees, and supplies. Think of everything you might spend money on such as a website, appreciation gifts to volunteers and special events. On the expense side, it is better allow more funds than not enough. It might be helpful to consult with other homeschool co-ops in your area or via the internet on their co-op expenses.

You could also ask the co-op's volunteer teachers to give the treasurer an estimate of their class expenses. I recommend that you follow the example of larger nonprofit organizations and churches that are structured into departments. Each department submits an estimate of expenses to the organization's treasurer. As a church treasurer for four years, I learned the importance of letting each department estimate their own expenses. You can practice the sample principle in your co-op at a simpler level. Have the treasurer ask each volunteer, teacher and committee for an estimate of expenses. With this data she will be ready for the next step of balancing a budget.

Compare and adjust

After income has been predicted and expenses have been estimated, the treasurer has the task of balancing the budget. Start by comparing total revenue to total expenses, and adjust the two until you have a balanced budget. I highly recommend planning for a small surplus as a protection for the unexpected. If you cannot balance your budget, you have two choices: cut expenses or increase income. You could recalculate your income by increasing membership dues. Try increasing dues 25% and then 50% until the budget balances. Also consider a fundraiser to bring in income. After increasing income as much as you can reasonably hope to accomplish, you may need to consider cutting expenses wherever you can. Go back to your volunteers and ask for a 10% or 20% reduction in their estimated expenses. Consider how to eliminate some projects, events or other areas of expense. Some groups find they must be better shoppers for supplies or request donations of classroom supplies to keep their expenses within the budget.

Examine the following sample budget for a homeschool co-op

Budget for Homeschool Co-op

Income

Contributions	$ 25
Co-op fees	$ 1250
Special Events	$ 50
Fundraiser	$ 100
Total Income	**$ 1425**

Expenses

Teacher Pay	$ 200
Rent	$ 500
Website fees	$ 100
Copies/Office	$ 150
Classroom Supplies	$ 200
Insurance	$ 125
Special Events	$ 100
Total Expenses	**$ 1375**

Net Income or Loss	**$ 50**

This budget shows a $50 surplus at the end of the year. Although this seems like a good plan, the co-op would barely be solvent if an unexpected expense arose. This organization also relies on contributions and fund raisers which are uncertain sources of income. If this organization does not increase their income or get a generous donation, they may not be able to cover their expenses. To remedy this potential situation, they could increase their co-op fees, recruit more families, or hold another fundraiser.

The Goal

The goal of budgeting is to plan the organization's sources of income as well as their expenses. Plan for a balanced budget and allow a small surplus for the unexpected. A remainder of 5% to 10% of budgeted income is helpful. When I served as co-op treasurer, we always planned for a small excess each year. One year we were very grateful for that cushion when we had an accident involving carpeting and printer ink. We rented a carpet cleaner and then hired a professional carpet cleaner to remove an ink stain. None of these expenses were in the budget, because it was an unexpected accident. The board even discussed the need to have the carpet replaced if the cleaner failed to fully remove the stain. We were able to consider that option because we had a financial cushion. Fortunately, the professional cleaner removed the stain to our great relief!

Bookkeeping Basics

There is no need to take a bookkeeping class in order to manage your co-op's finances. Instead there is a simple method that involves single entry bookkeeping, not double entry bookkeeping that is taught to accountants. Simply gather some lined paper or a computer spreadsheet and follow these easy steps:

1. List all your sources of revenue (income) and then all your expenses. This is called your chart of accounts. Here is an example:

Homeschool Co-op Chart of Accounts

Sources of Revenue:

Co-op dues

Fund raisers

Donations

Special events

Expenses:

Special events

Postage

Copies

Insurance

Website fees

Supplies (office, classroom and cleaning)

Rent

Refreshments

2. Take a stack of papers and give them titles for each item in your Chart of Accounts. If you are using a computer spreadsheet, then label different tabs on the worksheet for each expense or income category.

3. Make columns on each sheet. Label them "Date," then "Check Number" and finally "Description." In these columns you will record everything from your checking account and cash spending.

4. Total the entries once a month. The balances should then be transferred onto a statement of revenue and expenses. This report looks just like your budget except it shows the actual amounts received as income and spent on expenses rather than your estimates. The statement of revenue and expenses should have the same categories as your budget to make comparisons easy. I recommend that a statement of revenue and expenses be prepared monthly if the group is very active and collects large amounts of money. If the group is smaller with infrequent deposits and expenses, then the statement could be completed once every two or three months.

This system could be kept on a computer with a spreadsheet program like Excel or the free open-source version Open Office Chart (see www. OpenOffice.org). Individual worksheet tabs can be combined into a summary sheet called the statement of revenue and expenses. For easy comparisons, a column of the actual amounts can be lined up next to the budgeted amounts.

Using Personal Finance Software

Many mid-sized groups find that personal finance software (PFS) programs like Quicken and Microsoft Money are helpful for recording income and expenses. With this software creating a report is a very quick and easy. The programs are fairly easy to set up and may come already loaded on some computers.

I recommend you set up a Quicken or Money file just for the co-op, separate from your family's finances. Then set up accounts such as a checking account, savings account and cash account. Categories for the co-op will come from your chart of accounts. The set up may take a bit of time because PFS programs have categories like Groceries and Auto Loan that co-ops do not need. Fortunately it is simple to add and delete categories and customize the program to fit your needs. After arranging accounts and categories, enter checks and deposits just as you would do for your personal finances.

A medium homeschool co-op will be well positioned financially if they open a checking account, appoint a treasurer and create annual budgets. Keeping basic records on income and expenses will help the co-op remain solvent and relieve financial worries for the leadership team. If your group has already established these priorities, you may be ready to face more financial issues such as collecting fees, creating regular reports to the board and monitoring the budget more frequently. All these issues as well as computer record keeping are covered in the following section.

Large Group Management

Operating a large homeschool co-op is very much like running a business. There are fees to collect, bills to pay, insurance to purchase and perhaps employees to hire. Some of the issues a large homeschool organization needs to tackle include:

- Collecting fees

- Maintaining computer records

- Reporting regularly on financial status

- Monitoring the budget frequently

Collecting Fees

Although a small homeschool co-op may have difficulty collecting fees, a large homeschool group needs to pay extra attention to fee structure. In a small group, it is quite apparent if a family fails to make a payment, leaving invoices and payment tracking largely unnecessary. By the time your group grows to ten or twenty families, however, you need a system to record who has paid and the amount. When I took over as treasurer of our co-op, we had about thirty families. The fee structure was simple, because every family paid the same amount. However when I asked, "Do you record who has paid?" the leaders said, "Oh no, we just trust that everyone will pay." Although trust is a beautiful blessing in a co-op, records must be kept. The reasons include:

- People are forgetful. Sometimes I can't remember if I have paid my own co-op bill! Our co-op policy is that full payment must be received within the second week of meeting. There are usually two or three families that the treasurer has to track down because she had not received their payment. Usually, they have forgotten or misplaced the invoice in a pile of papers at home.

- Invoices track members' discounts. Some discounts may be given for extra effort. Some co-ops allow a director or other dedicated volunteer discounted co-op fees. In order to keep accurate record of discounts, I recommend the use of a paper invoice. An invoice (or bill) should show the full co-op fee and then list the discount subtracted from the fee, yielding the remaining balance.

- Some families may ask for progress payments. Although my co-op wants full payment up front, your group may have at least one family that would like to pay monthly or in installments. If it is manageable, try to accommodate them. Naturally, your treasurer must keep good records on how much they have paid and how much remains to be paid.

I recommend that your treasurer give out invoices for each student or family. A paper statement serves as a good reminder to pay the bill! If you use Quickbooks or other accounting software, you can easily print out invoices for each family. You might also record on a family's registration form that they have paid in full.

Computer Records

Even if you do not use a sophisticated computer program, a large homeschool co-op needs to use a computer spreadsheet to track their money at the very least. I discussed using a spreadsheet in the previous section on money management for a medium sized group. Many homeschool organizations find that using personal finance software programs such as Microsoft Money or Quicken work very well for record keeping. You might also consider using small business accounting software like Quickbooks or Microsoft's Small Business Accounting. These programs are used by millions of small businesses and are well suited to homeschool co-ops. Any accounting software program can help you:

- Print checks, pay bills and track income and expenses

- Create invoices, budgets and reports

- Track payroll and employee time

- Download credit card and bank transactions

- Track inventory and set reorder points

I would recommend using accounting software if you want to create invoices, sell inventory (like books or T- shirts) or pay employees. I have used Quickbooks for years as a co-op treasurer and find it essential for maintaining accurate records. To learn more about accounting software, visit my website, (www.HomeschoolCPA.com) for my e-book titled *Money Management for Homeschool Organizations*. I have a section in the e-book devoted to Quickbooks and Microsoft's Small Business Accounting packages.

Regular Reports

As part of its bylaws, a large homeschool organization should have a requirement that the treasurer make regular financial reports. More importantly, the leadership needs to hold the treasurer accountable. I worked with a homeschool co-op that frequently asked the treasurer for reports. The treasurer told them, "Everything is fine. We're in good shape." With other worries, the board completely trusted the treasurer and never asked for financial statements. After she resigned, the board realized that their finances were a mess! The treasurer had not been stealing or embezzling money but was merely sloppy. There were missing checks, no details on deposits, no records of who had paid, etc. It took a long time for the new treasurer to clean up the mess. In short, leaders should request regular, frequent financial statements.

Frequent Budget Monitoring

Your leadership team should regularly compare your actual financial condition to your budget. This comparison-to-budget report will look something like the statement of revenues and expenses but with an extra column for the budget. Some co-ops present all the information in one statement which is quite easy to do. If you have already input your budget figures, accounting software can quickly compile such a report.

Comparison of Actual Income and Expenses to Budget

Income	Actual	Budget
Contributions	$0	$ 25
Co-op fees	$1,300	$1,250
Special Events	$50	$50

Fundraiser	$ 100	$ 100
Total Income	**$1,450**	**$1,425**
Expenses		
Teacher Pay	$ 200	$ 200
Rent	$ 500	$ 500
Website fees	$ 100	$ 100
Copies/Office	$ 100	$ 150
Classroom Supplies	$ 228	$ 200
Insurance	$ 150	$ 125
Special Events	$ 130	$ 100
Total Expenses	**$1,408**	**$1,375**
Net Income or Loss	**$42**	**$50**

This homeschool co-op did fairly well and brought in more income than they expected. Conversely, they had a few areas where they overspent including classroom supplies, insurance and special events. Fortunately the co-op budgeted in a small cushion and still ended the year "in the black" with a small net income of $42.

If It's in the Budget, Can We Spend It?

I have volunteered as treasurer on several nonprofit boards. One board president honestly thought that if an expense was in the budget, then she could automatically spend that amount. I had to be fairly direct and remind her, *"Just because it's in the budget, doesn't mean it's in the checking account!"* She was spending money that hadn't yet arrived, believing that because "it was in the budget," she had full license to spend money.

Other directors that I have worked with loved to play around with the budget, thinking budgets were flexible, living things. I have heard, "Well, if we hold a fundraiser and bring in $500, can we buy the $500 computer?" I would remind the director that we had not yet met our fund raising goal for the year to cover budgeted expenses, let alone pay for additional items not included in the budget. A good treasurer will counteract overspending temptations by keeping accurate records and preparing financial statements, especially an actual-to-budget comparison.

More information

Managing money for any sized homeschool co-op is similar to managing the income and expenses of a business. A separate checking account will help manage the finances. Also, like in any business, it necessary to keep accurate financial records. The treasurer must stay on top of collecting income. Do your treasurer a favor and purchase software; it will make the job much easier. Using software, your treasurer will be able to quickly generate financial reports and answer the board's many questions about your co-op's finances.

On my website (www.HomeschoolCPA.com) I have an e-book titled *Money Management for Homeschool Organizations*. (An e-book is an electronic book that you can read on your computer screen and print out if you wish). This e-book has more details on

- Record keeping (with examples)

- Financial reports, including a sample invoice

- Comparing budget to actual spending reports

- How to read financial statements

- Using software like Quickbooks

In the e-book I also include chapters on two important issues that may affect your co-op's finances. The first discusses insurance for homeschool organizations and applies to any group concerned about potential accidents and liabilities. The other chapter concerns hiring paid teachers or other employees. Even a small homeschool group needs to know the employment laws concerning hiring and paying workers, as it is not as simple as one might think. You will want to tell your treasurer about this e-book because he or she will find it very useful in managing your co-op's money.

Chapter Nine:
Managing Volunteers and Conflict

One of the most challenging and rewarding parts of being in a homeschool co-op is managing other people! More than any other topic—including finances, curriculum, discipline, and dress codes—the number one problem faced by homeschool group leaders is inter-personal conflict. At the same time, the greatest blessings from homeschool co-ops come from friendships and the inter-personal connections made there!

Managing Volunteers

Everyone Cooperates

One piece of advice I consistently hear from successful homeschool co-op leaders is to *require commitment from the parents*. Repeatedly I hear comments like the following:

- Insist that everyone in the co-op work, whether they are teaching, helping, babysitting, or doing bookkeeping.

- A homeschool co-op requires members to co-operate, but this may not be easy

- A co-op where only some people volunteer is doomed to burn out those volunteers

- The atmosphere is truly cooperative if everyone helps out

Apparently successful co-ops have a very cooperative mindset. Ideally, members are inspired to have closeness and cooperation, much like the early Christian church described in Acts 2:44-47:

> *All the believers were together and had everything in common. Selling their possessions and goods, they gave to anyone as he had need. Every day they continued to meet together in the temple courts. They broke bread in their homes and ate together with glad and sincere hearts, praising God and enjoying the favor of all the people.*

Strive for a co-op that lives up to its name and is truly a cooperative effort. Your co-op could be an excellent witness for the Lord and for homeschooling, just like the early church. There is a lot of work to be done in running a homeschool co-op. The primary job in a co-op is that of the classroom teacher, but here are many other jobs to fill.

Volunteer teachers

Because most co-ops depend on the volunteer labor of homeschooling parents, many of the parents involved find themselves teaching or helping at some point. For example, I have taught Math Games, Personal Finance, and Career Exploration at my co-op. I have also found myself helping in sewing class, home economics, art, and the nursery.

Oftentimes, a volunteer teacher will run a classroom with a style that fits her personality. Some people are structured; others are more free spirited. Because I am quite organized and structured, I have my class plans all ready by the first day of class. Others in my co-op "go with the flow." Neither approach is right or wrong, just different. From my experience I have found that the free spirit mindset works much better with younger children than with high school students. Most high school students (and their parents) have expectations about what specific material to cover in a class. In order to cover the material in a timely way, high school students need a structured class. Some co-op directors let the less structured volunteers teach classes that are flexible such as gym, art or game-oriented classes, leaving the more methodic personalities to teach the more academic classes.

Maggie Hogan, a veteran homeschool parent, offers these wonderful suggestions in assigning volunteer teachers to specific classes:

> Choose teachers wisely. Just because someone is both willing and knowledgeable doesn't mean they will be good teachers. Questions to consider concerning teachers:
> - Do they like kids and have a good rapport with them?
> - Do they communicate effectively with both kids and parents?
> - Will they follow through?
> - Are they organized enough to do a good job?
> - Do they handle conflicts in a Biblical fashion?
> - Are they knowledgeable (or at least teachable) in the field they will be instructing? [27]

From my own experience, I would encourage a parent to belong to a co-op as a non-teaching member for at least a semester. While a new member should be given a volunteer job, she should not be entrusted with teaching too early. As she proves faithful in a little matter, she can be entrusted larger responsibilities as mentioned in Jesus' parable of the talents:

> *His master replied, 'Well done, good and faithful servant! You have been faithful with a few things; I will put you in charge of many things. Come and share your master's happiness!'* (Matthew 25:21)

One year my co-op was thrilled that a new member offered to teach two high school classes. Since she was new, no one knew her personality or her teaching capabilities very well. We were pleased with her generosity but we were soon disappointed, as she became overwhelmed with too many responsibilities. She was late to class, failed to grade homework and tests and didn't calculate grades. Her helper ended up taking over the classes when the volunteer teacher failed to show up. I hope your co-op can learn from our mistakes and not face a similar experience.

Volunteer Jobs

Not everyone in a homeschool co-op needs to be a volunteer teacher. There are many tasks to do. As much as homeschool co-ops vary, so do the possible volunteer positions. Common volunteer jobs include:

- Clean up crew
- Set up and tear down team
- Fund raising coordinator
- Nursery caregiver
- Lunch room or study hall monitors
- Field trip organizer
- Hospitality coordinator
- Registration director
- Building liaison
- Nurse
- Newsletter editor
- Website coordinator
- Special events planner
- Yearbook advisor

Most likely you can add more volunteer roles for the parents in your co-op:

_____

_____

_____

_____

_____

Can you pay a volunteer?

Many co-ops wonder if a volunteer can be paid. Sometimes a co-op may want to pay a generous volunteer who has given significant time to the homeschool organization. While co-op members work hard and deserve some show of appreciation, *volunteers* are not paid. When a person is paid, he is no longer a volunteer; he or she is (probably) an employee. Hiring an employee inevitably creates paperwork and tax filings. Usually a small homeschool group does not want to attend to W-2 forms, Social Security taxes or federal and state tax withholdings.

If a co-op leader or paid teacher is not an employee, he or she could be classified as an independent contractor which involves less paperwork and fewer tax filing requirements. Independent contractors are self-employed individuals that perform a specific task without supervision. They are typically small business owners. If your paid co-op director is not a small business owner and your board directs or controls her work, then she is not an independent contractor, but rather an employee of the co-op. The IRS has a 20-factor test to determine independent contractor status as well as a brochure *Independent Contractor or Employee* (Publication 1779) at http://www.irs.gov/pub/irs-pdf/p1779.pdf. Also visit my website (www.HomeschoolCPA.com) for the e-book *Money Management for Homeschool Organizations,* which includes information on hiring employees.

What can you do to show your appreciation in lieu of paying cash? Here are some ideas:

- Offer your hardworking volunteers a tuition discount or free membership in the co-op.

- Present a token of appreciation such as a gift certificate, flowers or chocolate!

- Offer to baby-sit her children so she has a day or night out.

- Share the burden of leadership by delegating some of the leadership tasks.

Try to avoid the cash payments as they will be taxable income for the recipient.

Paid teachers

Some co-ops desire to hire a paid instructor for some classes. My co-op has a guitar instructor that is paid directly by the parents for the classes he holds at our co-op. Other co-ops make heavy use of paid teachers as employees. Even if your co-op uses hired teachers, and parental involvement is limited, the parents should be asked to cooperate in the running of the co-op. One group describes the cooperation between parents and their paid tutors as follows:

> It is important for students, parents and tutors alike to realize that this is a unique partnership. All have come together for the common goal of educating teenagers and preparing them for whatever God has created them to do. Whereas sometimes in schools a teacher-student-parent relationship is seen as adversarial...this program is an actual partnership. We seek to uncover and bring out the best in each other.... We look forward to our partnership in the coming year. [28]

This program, called Providence Extension Program (PEP), is not a "true" co-op because the tutors are hired by the organization to teach classes instead of relying on volunteer parents. My daughters have been involved in PEP for several years. As a parent I am required to:

- pay my tuition
- buy textbooks
- get my child to class on time
- supervise my student's work
- provide at least five hours of volunteer time, either as a study hall monitor or in helping to clean the building

Demanding some volunteer effort is a typical requirement in extension programs. Homeschool extension programs differ from co-ops in that usually the teachers are hired and parental involvement is minimal. Another extension program describes itself:

> The LOL [Leaves of Learning] teen program has been a big success over the past 6 years. We attribute this success to the respectful, nurturing environment, small class sizes, caring facilitators and the students themselves. Leaves of Learning provides an opportunity for homeschoolers to enroll in some of those more difficult high school subjects, sometimes hard to teach at home, as well as enrichment classes such as art and drama. The quality of our classes in combination with the positive social environment at Leaves of Learning has filled a gap that has kept many homeschoolers from returning to traditional high school. In fact, we had our first home schooled senior class graduation in 2002.[29]

Leaves of Learning is a "drop off" homeschool extension program because the students come for classes and the parents do not stay and volunteer. Although the teachers are hired, the program still needs the help of parents. They require each family to contribute time or money:

> Family Jobs: The money we receive for tuition does not cover all our costs. We choose not to raise tuition as that would put our program out of reach for many of our families. Instead,

we absolutely depend on donations of either time or money (or both!) from our families. We require every family to take on a specific job, or to pay a $25 monthly fee. Families with students taking 3 hours or less per week pay $15 per month or have reduced job responsibilities.[30]

The possible volunteer jobs include cleaning (a very popular use of volunteer labor), drama production and fund raising.

Managing Conflict

Unfortunately, nearly all homeschool groups face conflict at some point. If you put a bunch of independent-minded, self-sufficient people in a room together, you will have differences and disagreements! Common causes of conflict include misunderstandings, usually due to poor communication and differing expectations, values or opinions. Sometimes competition over money, time or space can occur in homeschool circles and cause unrest. Also, sinful attitudes such as pride, greed and selfishness can cause discord.

The best way to manage conflict is to be proactive and keep tensions from growing. Many homeschool groups have instituted very clear policy manuals to avoid misunderstanding. Having conflict resolution policies and a clear mission statement can help everyone understand expectations and values. I have included a few samples of conflict resolution policies at the end of this chapter.

How to Manage Conflict in a Homeschool Co-op

Ken Sande, author of *The Peacemaker: A Biblical Guide to Resolving Personal Conflict*[31] points out that there are three ways to respond to conflict. Two of the methods, escape and attack, are inappropriate, leading to heartache and trouble. Escape involves denial or avoidance because some people prefer to avoid conflict rather than face it. They may believe conflict is wrong or dangerous. Conversely, attackers are more interested in winning than in restoring a relationship because they see conflict as a competition, a contest or a control issue. Attacking is frequently used by strong, confident people. Only the third method of conflict resolution, peacemaking, is the proper way to settle disputes. Peacemaking—which includes overlook, reconciliation, negotiation, mediation, arbitration and accountability—is the resolution method commanded by God. The goal of peacemaking is to preserve relationships and find a mutually agreeable solution.

Personal Peacemaking

Mr. Sande divides peacemaking into two areas: personal peacemaking and public peacemaking. The former means resolving conflict with the other party without making the dispute known publicly. Three aspects of personal peacemaking include overlooking an offense, reconciliation and negotiation.

Overlooking an offense: "*A man's wisdom gives him patience; it is to his glory to overlook an offense*" (Proverbs 19:11)

Sometimes an offense is small or unintentional and can be resolved by overlooking the wrong. Overlooking, which is a type of forgiveness, is a deliberate attempt not to dwell on an offense, talk about it or grow bitter over it. You may ask yourself, "Is it really worth fighting over?" and decide it is not. Overlooking an offense happens quite frequently in homeschool groups. So long as you are not keeping a mental record of offenses, overlooking them is an appropriate way to deal with conflict.

Reconciliation: "*If your brother has anything against you...go and be reconciled*" (Matthew 5:23-24)

Some offenses are too large to be overlooked, perhaps because a relationship has been painfully damaged. Reconciliation may involve confession on your part. Have you said something unkind? Have you gossiped about the person or problem? Have you tried to control others? Reconciliation is not merely confrontation, but is rather gently restoring the relationship. Ask for God's wisdom and a gentle spirit as you approach the other party you need to be reconciled with. Be clear and specific. Also consider using creativity through metaphors or stories to make your point.

Negotiation:

Although reconciliation frequently settles the personal side of a dispute, negotiation may be needed to work out any material issues such as money or property. Negotiation is a bargaining process to reach a settlement agreeable to both sides. With this method, it is important to first gather and focus on the facts of the dispute and then recognize the needs of each party. Be prepared with several options and anticipate the other party's reaction to your offer.

One woman shares her success with personal peacemaking in this wonderful story:

I remember many years ago when I was attending a church and put into a women's leadership position. One lady was not happy because I tried to turn the women's ministry into a ministry instead of a gossip session. She became bitter and started to tell many lies about me. To our face she was my friend, behind my back she was horrible. To make a long story short, God told me to start leaving her gifts (did I mention she was also my neighbor?) and so I did. I started to praise God for her everyday and at least twice a week I would leave something on her doorstep or mail it to her. Always anonymous. After about 3 months I noticed the lies had stopped and in 6 months she came to me asking for forgiveness. We became good friends after that and God brought total healing. She died after that but she had forgiveness in her heart and I sadly lost a friend. I learned many things through that very hard year, none of the lessons would I want to change. The biggest key was praising God for her (not asking God to change her) and investing in her life. My attitude was one of wanting God to get the victory and Praise the Lord, He did!! I have since applied these principles to various situations, in various ways. None have been as severe as the first one, but God has always used that situation to remind me how to handle it and to begin praising. Don't get me wrong, the praising isn't always from the heart when you start, but it must be from obedience.[32]

Notice how the woman's emphasis was on restoring a relationship and not on "winning" or being in control. She was able to resolve her conflict privately, but sometimes a conflict must be handled in a public forum.

Public peacemaking

Public peacemaking involves mediation, arbitration and accountability. Because these methods bring in outside parties to settle a dispute, they should be used only after personal peacemaking has been tried and has failed.

Mediation occurs when an objective, outside person is invited into a conflict. The goal of the mediator is to facilitate better communication and to explore possible solutions. Matthew 18:15-16 provides guidance for mediation:

> *"If your brother sins against you, go and show him his fault, just between the two of you. If he listens to you, you have won your brother over. But if he will not listen, take one or two others along, so that every matter may be established by the testimony of two or three witnesses."*

Homeschool groups can use mediation when needed. Here is one story of how a homeschool support group used mediation:

> Our support group experienced some interpersonal conflict this year. There had been some tension between a couple of members over a perceived slight and it suddenly escalated at a teen meeting when one of these moms started to criticize another, a leader, who wasn't present. She was stopped by third, who firmly took the conversation in a different direction.

What followed over the next 2 or 3 days was a series of e-mails and phone calls between four members that turned into a name-calling shouting match, with bitterness, anger, and deeply hurt feelings. I was called after this had all occurred, and talked to each person individually to try to sort out the truth. It was difficult because there was so much emotion and misunderstanding involved.

Obviously, this brought the leadership council for our support group to its knees (literally), and we spent a good bit of time individually and collectively in prayer. As a result of this, we are working on a revamped Code of Conduct for the group that includes sections on Behavior, Unity, Communication, and Reconciliation. One leader is writing a series of articles for our newsletter on peacemaking and biblical conflict resolution and Christian growth. We saw clearly that although we are a Christian support group, our members come from a variety of denominations and are in very different places in their walk with the Lord.

One wise father commented that we shouldn't be surprised when conflict occurs, especially in a large group like ours. We are all sinners who fall short of the glory of God. One member had exclaimed during this episode, "I expect this kind of thing in the school system. But I can't believe this kind of thing goes on in a Christian homeschool group!" Well, neither being a Christian nor being a homeschooler prevents us from falling into sin. But how we respond and deal with conflict is what people (including our children!) will watch and remember, and what will glorify our Lord or bring him shame.[33]

When this homeschool leader was brought in as a mediator, she spoke with wisdom to people both individually and collectively. She and her leadership team also prayed extensively, which certainly helped. Ultimately the goals of mediation—improved communication and development of solutions—were achieved.

Arbitration is another form of public peacemaking similar to mediation.

In this case, however, the arbitrator acts like a judge making a decision that is binding upon both parties. If your conflict has not been resolved through private peacemaking or mediation, I would recommend you wait before attempting arbitration. First read *The Peacemaker: A Biblical Guide to Resolving Personal Conflict* and contact Peacemaker Ministries (www.Peacemaker.net or www.HisPeace.org) which has unpaid volunteers who will act as arbitrators.

The final type of public peacemaking is **accountability** which involves following the commands of Matthew 18:17:

> *If he refuses to listen to them, tell it to the church*

This method should only be used when a professing Christian refuses to be reconciled. In homeschool groups this could mean deferring the conflict to the member's local pastor or church. Alternatively, the homeschool group may consider asking the offender to leave the group. Experienced homeschool leader Kim Wolf offers the following advice on using accountability in a homeschool group:

> Now, this can be sticky! Personally, on the third strike our board would come to her and ask her to kindly and quietly leave. We *may*, at the next support group meeting or in the newsletter, *lovingly* announce that because of a member's *choice* to cause dissension in the group, and she was asked in the spirit of Matt. 18:15-17 to stop; she *chose* not to stop and was kindly asked to leave. And leave it at that - no other explanation will be necessary for the general group.

> OK, here's the really down side: it is possible that she might spread malicious gossip about your group, but you will just have to pray about it, forgive her and correct the rumors when you can. But in the long run, you will be known by your fruit and the gossip should roll off of you all like rain on the newly waxed car![34]

Sample Conflict Resolution Policies

Most conflict resolution policies created by homeschool groups use Matthew Chapter 18 as a model. Hear how a few groups spell out their conflict resolution policies:

From The Learning Tree in Cincinnati, OH:

Unfortunately, personality conflicts and misunderstandings can happen. Though rare, it is important that we agree on how to deal with these situations should they arise.

The offended party must first seek to resolve conflict between the two parties. If either party is unsatisfied or resolution cannot be met, they then need to seek the assistance of an objective party (typically the Director or other member of the Leadership Team) to mediate.

If necessary, the conflict will be taken to the other members of the Leadership Team and they will make the final decision.[35]

From South Coast Christian Educators Ministries in California

Disputes: From time to time misunderstandings or hurt feelings can arise between members. When a conflict arises between you and another member, we ask that you follow biblical outlines. Be slow to anger, willing to overlook and offense, pray before you speak or act. Matthew 18 outlines a fine pattern for conflict resolution. Seek to speak to the person you have conflict with first. If a problem is still not settled, seek counsel from leadership. In most cases, disagreements are just that: disagreements. Moving on is usually the best course of action. Strive to be peacemakers.[36]

From Home Grown Kids in California

Mediation: Parents who are unable to resolve a conflict on their own will be referred to mediation. This is a group of three volunteers who agree to be fair and impartial in helping to resolve conflicts within the group. Should we ever need to call upon this group for conflict resolution, the volunteers will be chosen at random, by having their names drawn from a hat. There is a Yahoo Group database for members who wish to volunteer to be mediators. All members agree to abide by the decisions resulting from mediation. Anyone who is not willing to do so will be asked not to attend any group functions until he/she agrees.[37]

Conclusion

Peacemaking is the most successful technique to dealing with conflict resolution in your homeschool co-op. Encourage your members to settle disputes by overlooking an offense, reconciling differences and negotiating when needed. Develop a conflict resolution policy to guide you through public peacemaking methods such as mediation, arbitration and accountability.

Managing volunteers, paid teachers and conflicts can be exhausting to a homeschool group leader. To avoid frustration and burn out over these issues, consider having some policies that encourage everyone to contribute and cooperate. Read *The Peacemaker* by Ken Sande to understand how to deal with conflicts. Finally, educate your members and leadership team on appropriate method of solving conflicts peacefully.

Chapter Ten:
Ready for the Next Step?

The hardest thing to understand in the world is the income tax.

—Albert Einstein

Do You Need to Be a 501(c)(3) Tax-exempt Organization?

If you have already established a board, budget and bylaws, you may be considering whether your homeschool co-op is ready for the next step: gaining 501(c)(3) tax-exempt status with the Internal Revenue Service. While you may have heard terms like non-profit, tax-exempt and 501(c)(3), you may be wondering what government recognition could mean for your group—good and bad. What are the benefits? What will it cost in dollars and time? Is your group ready?

Becoming a formally recognized not-for-profit organization involves a lot of government paperwork. I have helped several homeschooling organizations obtain official not-for-profit status (known as 501(c)(3) status or "tax-exempt status" to the IRS). First, an organization must ask whether they desire the benefits of 501(c)(3) status and also determine if they are prepared to carry out the responsibilities involved in doing so.

Benefits of 501(c)(3) Status

Contributions

The greatest benefit of 501(c)(3) status is not for the charity, but for its donors. Any contributions of cash or property to a qualified charity are tax-deductible to the donor. This is a significant benefit and many organizations pursue the paperwork of 501(c)(3) status simply to receive more donations. If your homeschool co-op is not dependent upon receiving donations (i.e., if you are funded by solely by member fees), then you may not need to pursue the 501(c)(3) status. On the other hand, you may have individuals or businesses that wish to make donations, but will not do so unless the donation is tax deductible. In this case, you will need the IRS's coveted "qualified charity" status. Also, if you are seeking government or charitable foundation grants, 501(c)(3) status will be a requirement.

Special Programs

Some special programs, especially fundraising opportunities, are open only to 501(c)(3) organizations. My local grocery store's "Rewards Program" requires that a group be a 501(c)(3) tax-exempt organization; not even non-profit corporations registered by the state as charitable organizations qualify. Non-501(c)(3) organizations simply cannot participate. One homeschool co-op in my area applied for 501(c)(3) status just to participate in this fundraiser. Since it brings in $3,000 a year for them, it was worth the time and effort to become a 501(c)(3) tax-exempt organization.

In addition to store "reward" programs, our community has a discounted office supply store open only to 501(c)(3) organizations. While this store is a great place to buy inexpensive office supplies, furniture, and paper, they sell only to 501(c)(3) organizations. I have also seen large companies give away software and computers, but only to 501(c)(3) organizations.

Discounts

There are other desired benefits of 501(c)(3) status, including special discounts on postage, rent, equipment and some taxes. The US Postal Service offers a special reduced mailing rate to 501(c)(3) organizations. Some landlords and businesses will cut their rental rates for nonprofit organizations. Some states offer special status to nonprofits such as sales tax exemptions on purchases made by the nonprofit, while other states exempt nonprofits from property tax. Check with your state's attorney general's office to see if 501(c)(3) status is required for these benefits. Sometimes it is not needed; just being a nonprofit is enough.

Prestige

One of the intangible benefits of the 501(c)(3) status is prestige. When I see a nonprofit organization list that they are "a 501(c)(3) nonprofit organization," I know that they are serious in their mission. Because they have met the IRS requirements, they are well organized and have a solid financial system. I know that they expect to have some longevity, and they went to extra effort to be accountable. The 501(c)(3) status gives me assurance that the organization is trying to run a responsible organization.

Disadvantages of 501(c)(3) Status

While there are numerous benefits for obtaining 501(c)(3) status, the process involves impediments too. These disadvantages include fees, paperwork, government-imposed limitations, and annual reporting to the IRS and your state.

Cost

The costs to apply for 501(c)(3) tax-exempt status can accumulate. The application fee alone to the IRS is $300 for organizations with gross annual revenues under $10,000. The fee increases to $750 for organizations with gross annual revenues over $10,000. (Gross revenues are the total amount of income the organization brings in before subtracting expenses). In addition to the IRS fee, are the fees for state incorporation, which can vary widely. My home state of Ohio charges $150 for nonprofit incorporation, while our neighboring state Indiana charges only $30. Many organizations hire professional assistance from either a lawyer or an accountant to help them with the IRS application (Form 1023). These professional fees can range from $500 to $1500 or more. On my website, I compare prices for several professionals that assist nonprofits in the 501(c)(3) application process. Visit www. HomeschoolCPA.com and click on the Services page. My current fees are listed there also.

Paperwork

The paperwork to apply for 501(c)(3) status can be daunting. The application form for the IRS (Form 1023) is 28 pages long, while the instructions for this form are another 38 pages! In addition, Form 1023 asks for these documents:

* Bylaws
* Articles of Incorporation or "organizing documents"
* Policy manuals
* Mission or purpose statements
* Explanation of activities
* History of your organization
* List of board members' names and addresses
* Three years of financial statements
* List of donors and amounts donated

Because of the daunting amount of paperwork required, some organizations find they first need to spend time assembling the information before they can begin the 501(c)(3) application process.

Limitations

Some of the greatest drawbacks to 501(c)(3) tax-exempt status are the limitations the IRS imposes. Particularly limiting is the political involvement of 501(c)(3) organizations. The IRS prohibits qualified charities from engaging in certain political activities. While a 501(c)(3) organization can lobby for or against legislation, it cannot endorse a candidate for a local, state or federal office. Nonpartisan educational activities, however, are allowed.

Annual Reporting

Another disadvantage of 501(c)(3) status is the yearly reporting. Most 501(c)(3) organizations must file an annual information return called Form 990 with the IRS. This is not a tax return, because tax-exempt organizations are generally not required to pay income tax[38], but the form certainly looks like a tax return! The IRS asks detailed questions about activities, finances, fundraising, donations and board members. Fortunately organizations with annual revenues under $25,000 are exempt from filing this annual information return. Your homeschool group may be small enough to avoid this filing requirement. These reporting rules are also in a state of change as this book goes to press. For assistance in preparing a Form 990 Information Return for Tax-exempt Organizations, or learning the latest IRS reporting requirements, visit my website www.HomeschoolCPA.com.

Please do not let this list of disadvantages discourage you from pursuing 501(c)(3) status! I do not mean to discourage you, but I want to make you aware of the obstacles in the path ahead. Most groups find these limitations and disadvantages easily overcome and believe that the considerable advantages far outweigh the drawbacks.

501(c)(3) Status: Are You Ready?

The IRS application for 501(c)(3) tax-exempt status is not an easy process. In fact, the IRS designed it to be difficult! According to IRS statistics, about 70% of applications for tax-exempt status are not granted. This is usually because the applicants drop out of the system, not because the IRS rejects them. Actually the IRS approves 99% of applicants who complete the process. Normally, applicants abandon seeking tax-exempt status because they decide the process is not worth it and become discouraged by the IRS's questions and requests for more data. Sometimes, applicants cannot meet the IRS requirements for bylaws, board members' names, conflict of interest policies, etc. In order to have success with the 501(c)(3) application, your homeschool co-op must be organized. I have complied a checklist to determine if your organization is ready to apply for 501(c)(3) tax-exempt status:

Is Your Group Ready for 501(c)(3) application?

❑ Do you have a board of directors and a method to elect the board?

❑ Does your board meet regularly and keep minutes of your meetings?

❑ Do you have three years of financial history, or can you predict two years of budgeted financial statements?

❑ Do you have a mission statement?

❑ Would you be willing to forgo endorsing political candidates? (501(c)(3) organizations may not endorse political candidates)

❑ Do you have enough money to pay the IRS filing fee of either $300 or $750, a state incorporation fee and the cost of professional assistance if needed?

If you said no to any of these items, your organization is not yet ready for 501(c)(3) application. If you first work to prepare your group, become organized and gather the paperwork, then the application process will go smoothly.

Common Non Profit Formats

A nonprofit organization can exist in several different formats, from a simple, informal, unincorporated organization all the way to a large, structured, tax-exempt organization. To help you sort out the various terms, I have created this diagram. The bottom of the pyramid represents the least organized type of homeschool group. As you climb the pyramid, the structure increases by adopting bylaws, forming a board, obtaining nonprofit incorporation and ultimately applying for tax-exempt status.

Typically, homeschool groups start at the unincorporated level (at the base in the pyramid diagram). They may exist at that level for as long as they wish, progressing to another level only as their program and membership demands increase. By the top two levels homeschool organizations will engage with state and federal governmental agencies. At the state level, your organization will work with your secretary of state's office if you become a nonprofit corporation. At the uppermost level of the pyramid, your group will deal with the IRS if you desire 501(c)(3) tax-exempt status.

510c3 Tax-exempt Status
Large, board, bylaws, 3 year budget, incorporated

Non Profit Corporation
Medium or large size, board, bylaws, incorporated

Unincorporated Organization (formal)
Medium-sized, checking account, board, bylaws

Unincorporated Organization (informal)
Small, cash based, may be no board or bylaws

Nonprofit Incorporation

Before you apply for 501(c)(3) tax-exempt status, your organization should consider becoming a nonprofit corporation.

Incorporation: What is It?

When you started your homeschool organization you were considered an "unincorporated organization," a form in which groups can exist indefinitely. Becoming a corporation means that you are establishing a separate legal identity. Incorporation also allows your group to put "Inc." behind their name. In a sense incorporation is like progressing from a "Mom & Pop Store" to "Mom & Pop, Inc." The business operations may stay the same, but a separate, legal entity has been created. Incorporation is handled by your state government, usually the Secretary of State's Office.

Incorporation: Do You Need It?

There are several reasons why a homeschool co-op might consider becoming a nonprofit corporation. These include having a tax avoidance on a cash surplus, legal protection, hiring employees, buying real property, and desiring continued existence. If your homeschool co-op has a financial surplus at year-end, you should consider incorporating as a not-for-profit organization. Your state government will consider your group a profit-seeking venture until you notify them otherwise. Incorporating as a not-for-profit will legally establish your organization with your state and exempt you from taxes on your surplus.

Incorporation also allows you to legally protect your leadership. The corporation, rather than individuals, will be held liable for any legal or financial problems that may arise. The directors of a corporation have limited liability, meaning that if your corporation is blamed for someone's injury or loss, only the assets of the corporation—not your personal assets—will be at risk.

Other reasons to incorporate include buying property or hiring employees. If your co-op is incorporated then the corporation—not the individual leaders of the co-op—becomes the property owner or the employer. Also, a desire for the organization to exist beyond the current leadership may cause your organizations to consider nonprofit incorporation. When granting nonprofit incorporation, state governments usually require three board members, which helps the health and longevity of your group. Finally, if you think your organization may desire to become a IRS tax-exempt 501(c)(3) organization, you should become incorporated first.

What Does Incorporating Involve?

Primarily, the disadvantages to nonprofit incorporation are the cost and the official forms. The paperwork is usually fairly simple as most states require only a one-page form listing the legal name of the organization and the officers' names. I recommend drafting Articles of Incorporation, which formally describe your organization's purpose and structure. My website www.HomeschoolCPA.com has sample Articles of Incorporation for you to use. In addition your Secretary of State's office will have information on incorporating as a nonprofit organization. The fees for incorporating run from $10 to $400, while the process may take two to six weeks.

Becoming a non-profit corporation may be in your organization's future. There are some fees and minor paperwork involved, but the benefits are worthwhile, especially if you have a financial surplus, wish to have a separate legal identity or protect your leadership. Incorporation is also helpful if you plan to rent property or hire employees. Additionally, I recommend that organization seeking 501(c)(3) status with the IRS begin by seeking nonprofit incorporation status with their state.

Checklist for 501(c)(3) status

After assisting several homeschool organizations to achieve the highly desired 501(c)(3) "qualified charity" status, I created this checklist of tasks. Your organization may already have completed several of these steps and could be well on your way to IRS tax-exempt status.

❑ Choose a name for your nonprofit. (See Chapter Five) Research the IRS Charities web site (www.irs.gov/eo), the internet and your state's Secretary of State's Office to be sure your name has not already been taken.

❑ Choose a board of directors. Often only three people (a president/director, a treasurer and secretary) are needed, although it is better to have more members, including a vice-chair/director.

❑ Write Articles of Incorporation, including a statement of your purpose. See Chapter Five for help writing a mission statement and visit www. HomeschoolCPA.com for sample Articles of Incorporation.

❑ Incorporate as a nonprofit organization in your state. Submit Articles of Incorporation with the required fee to the appropriate office in your state government, which is usually the Secretary of State's Office.

❑ Obtain a federal Employer Identification Number (EIN) by submitting IRS Form SS-4. Go to www.irs.gov and search on "EIN." You can apply on-line.

❑ Develop organizational bylaws, the rules by which you will operate. See Chapter Five for sample bylaws.

❑ Hold your first board meeting. Vote to approve the bylaws.

❑ Set up a budget. (See Chapter Eight)

❑ Read all you can on filing for tax-exempt status. Review IRS Publication 557, instructions for filing for tax-exemption. Also see my list of resources at the end of this chapter.

❑ Have your board vote to apply for 501(c)(3) tax-exempt status.

❑ File IRS Form 1023. Pay filing fees of $750 if you anticipate having revenue of over $10,000 per year, or $300 if you anticipate having revenue of less than $10,000 per year.

❑ Register as a charity within your state, if required. See www. HurwittAssociates.com, a website that lists nonprofit filing requirements for each state.

Resources

The IRS has two helpful booklets: "Applying for the 501(c)(3) Tax-exempt Status" (Publication 4220) and "Compliance for 501(c)(3) Tax-exempt Organizations" (Publication 4221). These are available on the IRS website at www.irs.gov/eo or by telephoning 800-829-3676 for no cost. Also see these books for more assistance:

- *How to Form a Nonprofit Corporation* by Anthony Mancuso

- *Nonprofit Kit for Dummies* by Stan Hutton and Frances Phillips

- *Tax Exempt 501c3 Status for Homeschool Organizations* (an e-book) available at www.HomeschoolCPA.com.

Part Three:

Not Burning Out

Chapter Eleven:
Avoiding Burn out

Leader burn out can be a serious detriment to a homeschool co-op's success. No one can continue leading if she is exhausted by excessive demands on her time and energy. Too often a co-op will fall apart without its leader. The final chapter in this book is perhaps the most important topic facing homeschool co-op leaders: avoiding burn out.

Symptoms of Burn Out

Sometimes we do not recognize the symptoms of burn out because our everyday lives are very full. In addition to raising our children, running a home, maintaining our marriages, and serving God and our communities, homeschool leaders take on additional responsibilities. It is no wonder that leaders resign complaining of fatigue, depression and frustration. Common symptoms of burn out include:

- Loss of interest, vision or enthusiasm

- Neglect of your own children and their homeschool time.

- Increased complaints from your husband or children

- Frustration and feelings of failure

- Depression or constant negative feelings

- Moodiness, irritability or increased worry

- Health problems such as insomnia, headaches, frequent colds, physical exhaustion

- Declining performance

It is important to distinguish between temporary "busy-ness" or fatigue and full fledged burn out, which is accumulated strain and stress that affects other areas of your life. After nearly every co-op day, I feel exhausted. One fellow board member takes a nap after co-op, but she is only temporarily fatigued. We joke that we love when co-op starts, but we also love when it ends! A symptom of burn out would be the loss of the initial enjoyment and anticipation that co-op day should bring. I know that I am tired at the end of a long co-op day because I have invested so much into my students. I really enjoy teaching and I experience a "good" type of fatigue.

Ten Ways to Avoid Burn out

Throughout this book, I have included advice from homeschool co-op leaders. All their advice, if heeded, will help you avoid frustration, fatigue and stress. I have condensed their advice into a list that is easy to read. Feel free to share it with your fellow leaders so that you can hold one another accountable.

1. Approach the idea of leading a homeschool co-op with your eyes wide open. Know the advantages and disadvantages of co-oping. (Chapters One and Two)

2. Have clear and realistic expectations. Write down what you expect from a co-op experience. Read the section on Expectations in Chapter One.

3. Plan ahead. Have a mission statement. Decide what you will do, whom you will serve, as well as when and where you will meet. (Chapter Four)

4. Get help. You cannot do this alone. If you try to do it all, you will be exhausted and frustrated. (Chapter Six)

5. Focus on your purpose. You cannot be all things for all people. See Chapter Five for help in writing a mission statement and defining your purpose as a group.

6. Make policies. Written procedures will help the group rely on a plan instead of quick decisions made while in a crisis. Chapter Six has some ideas on policies.

7. Create a budget. Mismanaging money can be the downfall of a homeschool organization. Have a plan of where the money will come from and where it will go. Be sure to include a buffer for the unexpected. See Chapter Eight for help in establishing a budget.

8. Be prepared for conflict. You will have disagreements in any group of people. If you manage disagreements in a biblical way, conflict can strengthen your group. Chapter Nine has advice on conflict resolution.

9. Learn to manage volunteers. You will be working with volunteer teachers and parents. Delegate tasks to them that fit their skills. Do not try to do everything yourself. Read Chapter Nine for advice.

10. Pray and ask God for help. Jesus told his disciples,

> *Ask and it will be given to you; seek and you will find; knock and the door will be opened to you. For everyone who asks receives; he who seeks finds; and to him who knocks, the door will be opened* (Matthew 7:7).

God invites His people to ask for His wisdom, discernment and
help. Why not take advantage of the offer and ask for help?

Don't Do it All Yourself

A good leader does not try to do everything by herself, but rather
she leads by delegation. A homeschool leader needs to pass out
responsibilities to other members so that the co-op will run efficiently.
Here are a few ideas that co-ops have tried to delegate responsibilities:

- Discourage your director from taking on additional teaching
responsibilities. In my co-op, we freed our director from teaching
so that she could be available to handle co-op issues during the
co-op day. In the past we had leaders that loved to teach but were
unapproachable during their class time. Instead, our leader is now
free to walk the halls and look in on every classroom. She assesses
the needs of the teachers and students as she visits each room.
She captures the "pulse" of the co-op by being freed from other
responsibilities.

- The positions of director and treasurer should be split between
two different people. As I discussed in the chapter on money
management, this division of labor has several benefits. Although
avoiding mistakes and embezzlement were mentioned, an important
reason to split these tasks is to share the workload.

- A homeschool co-op board should assist the leader or director
in making decisions. Handling decisions should not be the sole
responsibility of one person. Trying to "call all the shots" was one
of the mistakes that Moses made, as I discussed in Chapter Six on
leadership. A director should be free to make small determinations
based on the group's policy manual, but topics outside the scope of
the written policies should be discussed with the board. Recently
my co-op arranged to have our board meetings during co-op hours.
It was an excellent decision because we made more decisions as a
group and took some responsibility off of our leader's shoulders.

- Lovingly approach your leader if she is taking on too much responsibility. At times our co-op board has been more than happy to let the director do everything. Unfortunately, we hastened her burn out by not encouraging her to delegate responsibilities. Now we have learned that if someone has an idea for a new activity, we ask the membership for a volunteer to head up the project. If there are no volunteers, the new activity never happens. As a board and as a co-op leader, your job is to oversee others in doing their jobs but not to do everything yourself.

Three Building Blocks for Success

Out of all the limitless advice regarding leading a homeschool co-op, the three most important items can be summarized in the ABC's of successful homeschool co-ops.

ABCs of Successful Homeschool Organizations

A Board: Follow the biblical example of Moses, who could not handle the burden of leadership alone. God directed Moses to:

> *"Bring me seventy of Israel's elders who are known to you as leaders and officials among the people... They will help you carry the burden of the people so that you will not have to carry it alone." (Numbers 11:16)*

You should do the same and establish a board of directors. Choose people of integrity with gifts of organization and discernment.

Bylaws: One of the first jobs of the board is to write out your bylaws. These are the general guidelines of the organization. Your bylaws should cover such issues as: membership, voting, meetings and officer positions. Also include a focused, clear mission statement in your bylaws.

Create a Budget: Your organization should prepare a budget before your program year starts. Predict your sources of income (dues, class fees, fundraisers, etc). Next estimate expenses such as postage, copying, building use fees and supplies. Compare income to expenses and adjust until you have a balanced budget or even a small surplus as protection for the unexpected.

Summary

The advice given in this book and summarized in this chapter should help you to be a successful homeschool co-op leader. Starting a homeschool co-op may be one of the greatest experiences of your life. My desire is that you look back on your co-op experience with fond memories. I hope you make wonderful friendships, bless many families and encourage children to love learning. Belonging to a homeschool co-op can be the salvation of many frustrated and lonely homeschooling mothers and may encourage some families to stay homeschooling that otherwise might "drop out." Some visionaries see co-oping as a means to help the homeschool movement grow and bless future generations.

As bountiful as the blessings of homeschooling and co-ops are, leading a homeschool co-op should never become your sole focus. If you find yourself suffering from the symptoms of burn out because you are serving others, you are over-committed. Follow the advice given in this chapter and delegate responsibilities to others. You will be happier, more relaxed and a better, stronger leader if you do not try to do everything yourself. I wish you the best of success!

About the Author

Carol L. Topp, CPA, is both an accountant and a homeschooling mother. She earned her Bachelor of Science degree from Purdue University and worked as a Cost Analyst for the US Navy for ten years. In 2000, Carol passed the Certified Public Accountant (CPA) examination. Carol has been homeschooling her two teenage daughters since they started first grade. She has been very active in her local homeschool community teaching classes and speaking at support group meetings. She has been a member of the Mason Ohio Homeschool Co-op since 2002 and volunteered as their treasurer for four years.

As an accountant, Carol has served on several not-for-profit boards as well as advising numerous homeschool organizations. She has expanded her work with homeschool groups to help several organizations obtain 501(c)(3) tax-exempt status. In addition, Carol has prepared annual Form 990 reporting with the Internal Revenue Service (IRS) for several homeschool groups. In 2006, Carol launched her website www. HomeschoolCPA.com to help homeschool organizations with annual reporting to the IRS as well as obtaining 501(c)(3) status.

Carol's publications include numerous articles and e-books about operating homeschool nonprofits. Her articles have appeared in *The Old Schoolhouse*, *Home Education* and *Home School Enrichment* magazines. In addition, Carol has enjoyed conducting workshops for homeschool leaders.

As a professional accountant, Carol's affiliations include the Ohio Society of CPAs, The Society for Nonprofit Organizations, the National Association of Tax Professionals, The Ohio Society of CPAs Speakers Bureau, and The Ohio Society's Not-for-Profit Section.

Residing in Cincinnati, Ohio, with her husband and two daughters, Carol enjoys reading, traveling, and homeschooling. Carol can be contacted through her website www.HomeschoolCPA.com

Visit my website

www.HomeschoolCPA.com

On the site you'll find:

- Articles about
    - starting a homeschool organization
    - leading a homeschool group
    - writing a mission statement
    - insurance

- Sample
    - Bylaws
    - Articles of Incorporation

- Questions & Answers from other homeschool leaders on
    - Raising money
    - Paying volunteers
    - Hiring teachers
    - Becoming a nonprofit

- E-books about
    - Money Management for Homeschool Organizations
    - Tax exempt 501c3status for Homeschool Organizations

- Subscription to the helpful quarterly newsletter *Homeschool Leader*

Endnotes

1 Hogan, Maggie, "Co-ops: The Inside Scoop", http://www.brightideaspress.com/articles/co-op2.htm

2 Gatto, John Taylor, *Dumbing Us Down*, (New Society Publishers, 2002)

3 Bray, Robyn," The Story of Two Desperate, Burned Out Homeschool Moms", http://www.geocities.com/braylink2772/DESPERATE.html

4 Bray, Robin

5 Bray, Robin

6 Calsbeek, Janine, "I Couldn't Believe All the Bones...", http://www.homeedmag.com/HEM/216/bones.html

7 Jew, Laurel, "How Does Your Co-op Grow?", http://www.welltrainedmind.com/coop.php

8 Bray, Robyn, "Operation Cooperation", http://www.geocities.com/braylink2772/OPERATION.html

9 Bell, Debra, "Family Schools", http://www.hsrc.com/Undefined/family_schools.htm

10 Bell, Debra

11 Jew, Laurel

12 Bell, Debra

13 Ramona Voight, e-mail to the author, September 13, 2006

14 TOSHSN_Leadership_Group http://groups.yahoo.com/group/TOSHSN_Leadership_Group/message/1213 June 23, 2006.

15 TOSHSN_Leadership_Group http://groups.yahoo.com/group/TOSHSN_Leadership_Group/message/1959. Sept 6, 2007.

16 Home Education Magazine. Jan-Feb 2004. "It's Perpetual Recess!" http://www.homeedmag.com/HEM/211/jfrecess.html

17 TOSHSN_Leadership_Group http://groups.yahoo.com/group/TOSHSN_Leadership_Group/message/1212 June 23, 2006.

18 TOSHSN_Leaders_Group http://groups.yahoo.com/group/TOSHSN_Leadership_Group/message/1160 May 26, 2006

19 Constitution of Bellevue Home School Enrichment Program, http://www.enrichmentbhse.com/Constitution.html

20 Christian Home Educators of Ohio, http://www.cheohome.org/Archived%20Articles/cheo_on_cyber_schools.htm

21 Homeschool Co-op Statements of Faith, http://www.eadshome.com/statementfaith.htm

22 Desert Hills Christian Homeschoolers Statement of Faith http://www.dhch.org/wst_page2.html

23 Homeschoolers of Wyoming Statement of Faith, http://www.homeschoolersofwy.org/faith.asp

24 Helping Hands Homeschool Co-op, http://www.helpinghandshomeschoolco-op.org/printables/statement_of_faith.pdf

25 Homeschool Enrichment Program, "Classes Taught Previous Semesters", http://www.hepcoop.com/previousclasses.html.

26 TOSHSN_Leadership_Group, http://groups.yahoo.com/group/TOSHSN_Leadership_Group/message/1952, Aug 11, 2007.

27 Hogan, Maggie

28 Providence Extension Program, "Parent Handbook: Partnership", http://www.pep1.org/docs/site1/Parents%20Handbook%202007-08.pdf

29 Leaves of Learning, "About Our Teen Program", http://www.leavesoflearning.org/teenhome.asp

30 Leaves of Learning, "Tuition and Fees", http://www.leavesoflearning.org/Tuition.asp

31 Sande, Ken. *The Peacemaker: A Biblical Guide to Resolving Personal Conflict*, (Grand Rapids: Baker Books, 2004)

32 TOSHSN_Leadership_Group http://groups.yahoo.com/group/TOSHSN_Leadership_Group/message/1827. April 26, 2007.

33 TOSHSN_Leadership_Group http://groups.yahoo.com/group/TOSHSN_Leadership_Group/message/1833 April 27, 2007.

34 TOSHSN_Leadership_Group http://groups.yahoo.com/group/TOSHSN_Leadership_Group/message/1572 November 28, 2006.

35 The Learning Tree Handbook, "Conflict Resolution", http://www.learningtreeonline.org/handbook.htm#Conflict%20Resolution

36 South Coast Christian Home Educators Policies, www.scchomeeducators.org/policies.htm

37 Homegrown Kids, www.homegrownkids.org/guidelines.html

38 501(c)(3) organizations do not pay tax on their exempt function income. If they have income from sources unrelated to their exempt purpose, they may be subject to an unrelated business income tax (UBIT).

Index

CPSIA information can be obtained at www.ICGtesting.com
Printed in the USA
BVOW032054201112

306075BV00007B/56/P